DEANE'S

SUBMARINE RESEARCHES

Submarine Researches

on the wrecks of His Majesty's late ships
Royal George, Boyne, and others,

by

Mr. C. A. Deane,

in his improved diving apparatus

With an Introduction by John Bevan, Ph.D., F.S.U.T.
Edited by Michael Fardell and Nigel Phillips

London:
The Historical Diving Society
2001

Limited to 750 copies,

of which this is

No. 589

The introduction © John Bevan

ISBN 1 900496 14 3

Designed and produced by Kitzinger, London
Printed and bound by Smith Settle, Otley

The publication of this book

has been made possible by the generosity of

Kerr-McGee Oil

explorers for North Sea oil

and the first company to produce oil from a well

out of sight of land.

INTRODUCTION

by John Bevan, Ph.D., F.S.U.T.

Charles Deane and his brother John were the inventors of a safe helmet-diving system, which was the first diving system (other than the diving bell) to enable a man to make a prolonged dive into deep water. The two brothers were the first professional helmet divers, and they demonstrated the versatility and merits of such an underwater breathing apparatus. Their design was the forerunner of the apparatus which became the 'standard' diving dress, in use by military and civilian divers throughout the world, and they can be rightfully credited with being the founding fathers of today's diving industry. *Submarine Researches* is the only book that Charles Deane published, and it is the first book to depict the use of the diving helmet and dress.

THE LIFE OF CHARLES DEANE

Charles Anthony Deane was the second of nine children, and the eldest son, born to John and Eleanor Deane at their home at 53 Hughes Fields, Deptford, Kent. Charles was baptised at St Nicholas' Church, Deptford on 2 October 1796. John Deane, the fourth child, was born on 6 April 1800.[1]

As Charles's father had served at sea in ships of the East India Company, he was able to have his sons educated free of charge at the Royal Hospital School, Greenwich, (now the National Maritime Museum) as 'objects of charity', and that is where both Charles and John received their formal education. Charles entered at the age of eleven on 18 November 1807, and left three years later on 30 August 1810, to seek an apprenticeship. After about three months, and at the tender age of fourteen, he was bound apprentice to the captain of an 80-ton vessel, the *Ceres*, which was employed in the coasting trade. Seven years later in 1817, at the age of twenty-one, his apprenticeship was complete.

That year he married Sophia McIntosh at the church of St Martin's in the Fields, on 25 May. They moved into a small house in New Street, next to Hughes Fields where Charles's parents still lived, and on 2 September 1818 their first child was born. He was baptised Charles Anthony, after his father, who was not present as he had found employment as a caulker on an East Indiaman, the *Warren Hastings*, and had sailed the previous May for India and China. Charles undoubtedly managed to get this job through his younger brother John, who had been serving on the same ship for the previous four years as the captain's servant. Charles made two trips to the Far East on the *Warren Hastings* before giving up the life of a sailor. His second trip ended in May 1820.[2] He was now more secure financially, and was able to buy a slightly larger house at no. 2 Charles Street in Deptford. He was also able to obtain a job as a caulker in Barnard's shipyard, Deptford.

1. The biographies of Charles and John Deane are covered in detail by John Bevan in *The Infernal Diver*, London, Submex Ltd., 1996.
2. India Office L/MAR/B/9 OO.

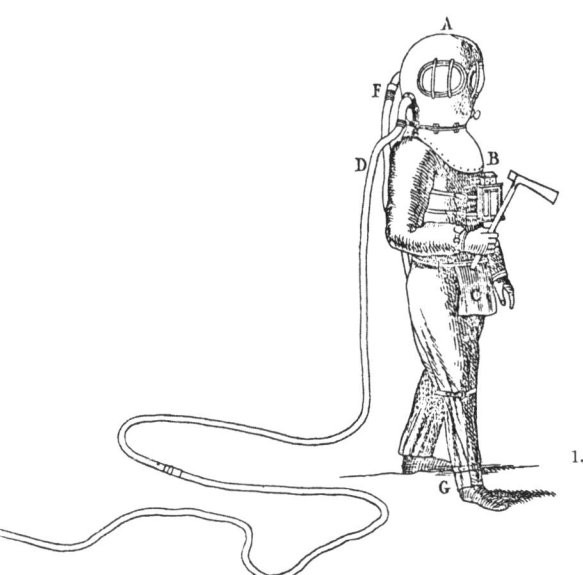

1. The illustration of the smoke helmet and dress filed with the patent application.

It was at this time that the inventive side of his complex personality began to express itself. On 20 November 1823 he took out a patent[3] for a smoke helmet which he had invented. This comprised a leather suit and a helmet fitted with three glasses. Two pipes were attached to the helmet, one to supply fresh air pumped from a bellows, the other, which was strapped down to the wearer's ankle, to remove stale air. In 1829 John Deane gave a spectacular demonstration of an improved version of this apparatus before the Society for Preventing the Loss of Life by Fire.[4] It was used extensively by fire-fighting services both in England and abroad.[5] On 15 May 1824, about a month after he enrolled the specification, Charles assigned the patent to his employer Edward George Barnard,[6] for which he received a generous payment of £417. He was now twenty-seven, and on the crest of a wave.

Meanwhile his brother John's seagoing career with the East India Company came to an end when he returned home in June 1826. Still a single man, he spent much of the next couple of years working with boatmen in Whitstable, who had developed a well-deserved reputation as expert salvors. Their routine work was sweeping for abandoned anchors and cables in the extensive roads in the Thames estuary, but greater rewards came from the salvage of cargo from the frequent shipwrecks, as well as from the salvage of the vessels themselves. They were so expert in this art that they were regularly commissioned by Lloyd's of London to recover cargo from wrecks all around the country, and abroad. There was also a thriving smuggling industry which exploited the clever concealment and recovery of contraband from the sea bed.[7] In fact his friend William Bell, an eminent Whitstable boatman and salvage expert, actually bought a diving bell at this time,[8] to try to expand his salvage work.

3. Patent Number 4869, *An Apparatus or Machine to be Worn by Persons Entering Rooms or other Places filled with Smoke or other Vapour, for the purpose of Extinguishing Fire or Extricating Persons or Property therein*; filed 4 November 1823; Specifications enrolled 1 April 1824.

4. *The Register of Arts and Journal of Patent Inventions*, London, 1829, vol. 3, pp. 184 and 234.

5. C. F. T. Young, *Fires, fire engines, and fire brigades*, London, 1866, p. 44.

6. Public Record Office, C33/865/4493.

7. R. H. Goodsall, *Whitstable, Swalecliffe & Seasalter*, 1938, pp. 261–262.

8. *Kentish Gazette*, 23 May 1828.

All these activities demanded expert seamanship, daring, and the ability to improvise. Over the years, a range of ingenious tools and techniques had been developed to recover material from the sea and out of the holds of sunken ships, but there was a continuous demand for improvement. Their methods were still rather crude and often ineffective. It would have been a difficult and frustrating task to attach a line to an abandoned anchor in forty feet of water a mile off shore in the Thames estuary. If it were only possible to get down there, it would have been such a simple matter to tie a rope to the anchor. John Deane knew how the diving bells worked in the Thames, with their air supplied by a force pump via an air hose; he also knew about his brother's smoke helmet, with its air supplied by a hose connected to a pump. In retrospect it appears a simple step to convert the smoke helmet to operate like a small diving bell.

The two Deane brothers began to experiment with diving apparatus, using a modification of the smoke helmet. The idea for doing so may have been John Deane's, and certainly it was only with his considerable assistance and initiative that the smoke helmet was modified and adapted for use under water. Within twelve months they had jointly developed their first fully operational diving helmet system. Their first trials were in the Croydon Canal, near Charles's home in Deptford. By the end of 1828, they had brought their diving helmet and dress to 'full perfection'.[9]

The operating principle of the Deane diving helmet and dress was extremely simple. The helmet worked in exactly the same manner as the common diving bell — it trapped a bubble of air around the diver's head. It is now often referred to as the 'open helmet' or 'open dress', because the bottom of the helmet was open to the water; the air venting from the helmet would have simply bubbled out from under the edges of the corselet, or breastplate. (A later modification introduced by others involved sealing the lower edge of the corselet to the water-tight suit, thus creating the 'close dress'.) The air was constantly replenished through an air hose from a force pump at the surface, in exactly the same way as the diving bell. It is remarkable that the open dress was not invented earlier than 1828, as diving bells had been operating on this principle since 1788, when Smeaton had first used a force pump to send air via an air hose to a diving bell in Ramsgate harbour.

The Deanes experimented with various attachments to the lower edge of the helmet, which included short jackets, or a simple skirt round the edge of the corselet. One piece of equipment which they introduced was the waterproof 'Macintosh' diving suit.[10] This was a one-piece suit, covering the whole body. The diver entered through the neck, and the feet were integral to the suit. It was made watertight at the wrists by tightly wound bandages. The wide neck was gathered up round the diver's neck and tied with a handkerchief. A canvas jacket and trousers were then worn over the expensive waterproof suit to give it protection, minimising wear and tear. Shoes with lead soles were

9. John Deane, in Henry Slight's *True Stories of HM Ship Royal George*, Ryde, 1841, p. 83.
10. The process by which rubber is dissolved and then used to waterproof fabric was invented by the Edinburgh surgeon James Syme. The process was taken up and patented by Charles Macintosh & Co. in 1823.

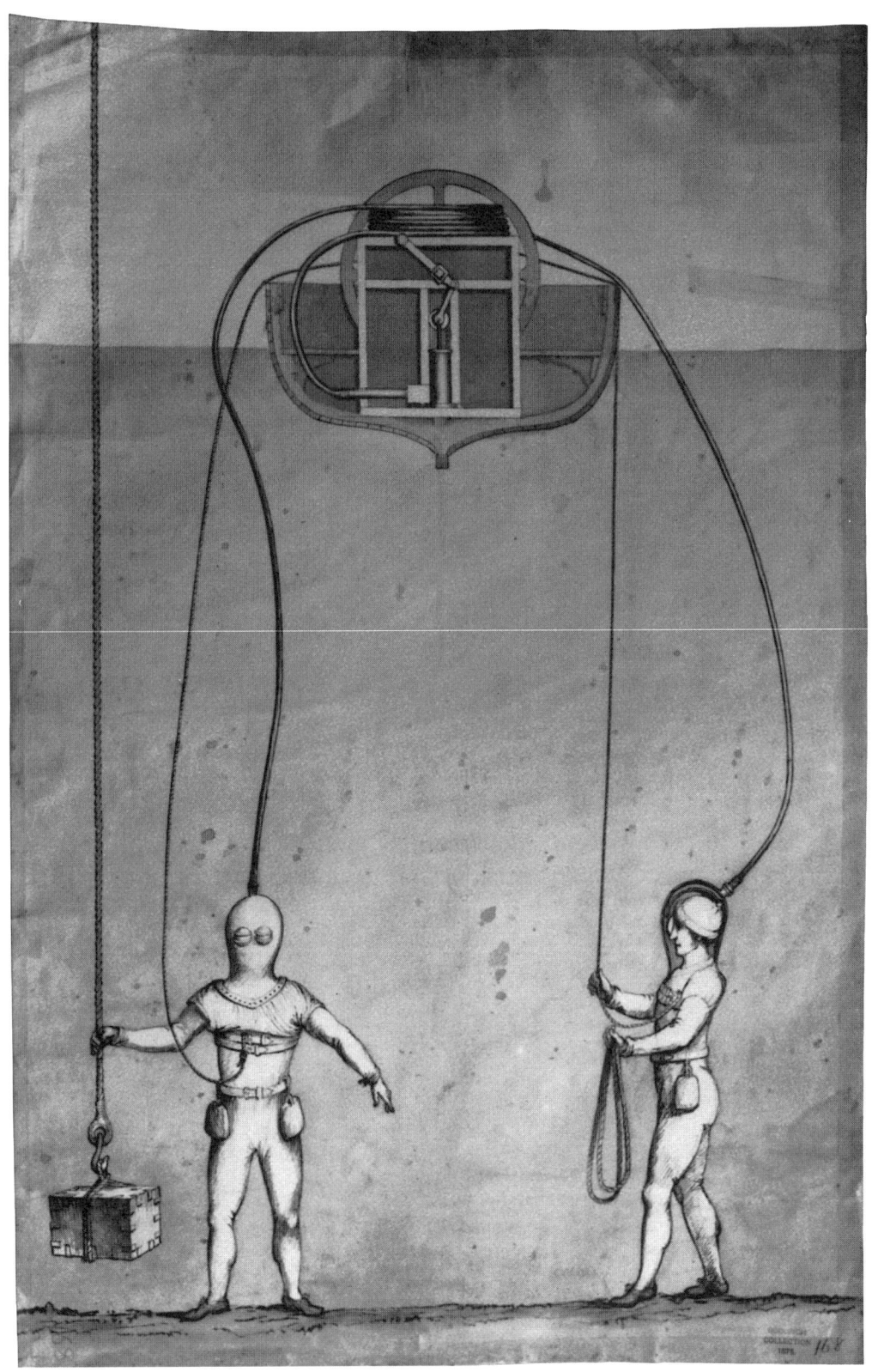

2. 'Simon Goodrich and his works as an engineer', Drawing Number 168, Science
    Museum Library, London.

strapped on the diver's feet, and the helmet was placed over his head. Finally, two large lead weights were hung over his shoulders, front and back. In general outward appearance, the diving helmet changed little over the ensuing 170 years or so.

The first opportunity the Deane brothers had of applying their new helmet commercially came in August 1829. Through the Whitstable connection with Lloyd's of London, they were invited to try out their equipment on the wreck of the East India Company's ship *Carn Brea Castle*, which ran ashore on the infamous 'back of the Wight' (the south coast of the Isle of Wight), the grave-yard of many a ship. The wreck was more or less intact, but had suffered dam-age to the hull, and her holds were completely flooded. The Deanes were able to use their diving equipment successfully to work under water, inside the holds, and to recover most of its valuable cargo, including several tons of cop-per. This is the first of their operations to be featured in *Submarine Researches*, which chronicles the next seven years of Charles's diving exploits.

The following year, Charles threw himself into marketing his new industry. He carried out demonstration dives for the Admiralty at Portsmouth and at Sheerness, and gave public demonstrations in London near Southwark Bridge and off Greenwich. It was about this time, when Charles demonstrated his diving apparatus to the Admiralty, that Simon Goodrich (1773–1847), the Engineer and Mechanist to the Royal Navy who was based at Portsmouth Dockyard, produced what is perhaps the best illustration of the early Deane diving dress (figure 2).

On a return visit to Portsmouth in 1832 with his brother John, Charles carried out some salvage work on the shallow wreck of HMS *Boyne*, just off Southsea beach. A ship of ninety-eight guns, the *Boyne* was undergoing repairs at Spithead in 1795 when she caught fire. Contemporary accounts suggest that the most likely cause was wadding from a marine's rifle (they were practising to windward) being blown back through the open windows of the admiral's cabin. She drifted to a position opposite Southsea Castle, where she blew up at 5 p.m., and sank.[11]

Perhaps most famously, in 1832 they carried out their first dives on the wreck of HMS *Royal George*, which capsized and sank in about 90 feet of water on 29 August 1782 at Spithead. Charles had acquired the rights to dive on the *Royal George*, and to salvage it, from the Admiralty and Board of Ordnance earlier in the year, and John Deane was effectively working as a sub-contractor to his elder brother. This was such a great achievement that Charles commissioned an engraving of the exploit, showing him diving on the bowsprit of this 100-gun warship (figure 3). The event also attracted the attention of Captain Basil Hall, a regular contributor to the *Nautical Magazine*, and he wrote a description of the Deanes' activities which was published in September 1832.[12] The article included one of the rare and valuable illustrations of the Deane diving helmet (figure 4). This version of the helmet featured a short tube tied to the side of the helmet, which was actually an experimental arrangement for venting the air

11. See *The Destruction of the Boyne, First Rate Man of War, of ninety-eight guns, by a most rapid and tremendous fire . . . on . . . May 4, 1795*. London: [c. 1810].
12. *Nautical Magazine*, September 1832, p. 359.

3. Detail from *A Representation of H.M.S. Royal George of 108 Guns*, a lithograph published in 1833.

from the helmet, probably when it was used with a long-sleeved jacket; it does not appear to have been incorporated into the Deanes' later helmets. In use, the tube would have been attached to the front of the diver's chest.

At the end of that year, Charles carried out an underwater structural survey of Blackfriars Bridge, on the Thames, for the eminent civil engineers Walker and Burges. The diving helmet had now been introduced to civil engineering.

In 1836 Charles's life began to take a turn for the worse. Tragically, his wife Sophia died that December after giving birth to their tenth child, Alfred, who died six months later. Two more of his children had also died young. Charles

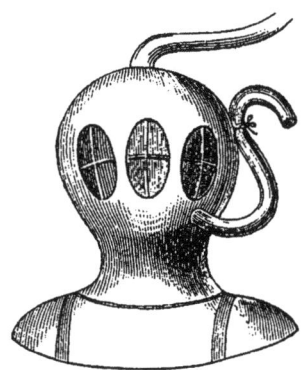

4.   The illustration of the helmet from
     the *Nautical Magazine.*

appears to have separated from his remaining family at that time, with his
older sister Maria helping out with the family affairs. At the same time a serious rift opened between him and his brother. In November of that year
Charles went down on the last dive he is known to have made, on the wreck of
the East India Company's ship *Venerable* in Torbay, Devon. From then on
Charles's life deteriorated rapidly.

The following year, two more of his daughters, Royal Georginia and Jane
(both aged two years) died during a typhus epidemic. It was perhaps prophetic
that the daughter whom he had named after the wreck which he had hoped
would make his fortune (the *Royal George*) was so cruelly snatched from him.
A year later, the wreck itself was also snatched from him just as he had been
planning to open it up with explosives. Colonel Pasley of the Royal Engineers
had become involved in underwater demolition in 1837, when the Port of
London Authority asked the Board of Ordnance to destroy a hazardous wreck
in the River Thames. The matter was referred to Pasley, who destroyed the
wreck in 1838.[13] He used his influence and high connections to wrest the rights
to work on the *Royal George* away from the civilian, Charles Deane.[14] Charles
pleaded passionately and emotionally with the Admiralty to prevent Pasley
from taking the *Royal George* away from him, but in vain.[15] Also in 1838, the
patent for his smoke helmet expired and any tenuous protection it may have
provided to the diving helmet version was lost for ever.

Charles was obviously under a tremendous strain throughout this period,
and it is perhaps not surprising that in 1839 he was confined for a period in
Peckham Lunatic Asylum, and registered as insane.

After his release he seems to have roamed the docklands of London's east
end, living in miserable, rented accommodation. He appears to have been trying to make a living as an inventor, but he had no success whatsoever. Salva-
tion almost arrived in 1844 when he successfully applied for, and received, a
grant from the Treasury in recognition of his contribution to the invention
and development of the diving helmet and dress, which by then had been
adopted by the Royal Engineers.[16] The award was the subject of a bitter dispute
between the two brothers as John applied to have a share. His claim was

13. 'Demolition of the Brig William', file of correspondence in the library of Royal Engineers'
Institution.
14. Public Record Office, WO 44/614, Engineer, 39, 282/1, 20 March 1839.
15. Public Record Office, ADM 1/4549, Pro D 71, 31 March 1839.
16. Public Record Office, 12/416, T1/4908, Treasury Paper, In, 27 July 1843.

referred to Colonel Pasley, but as Pasley did not fully appreciate John's contribution to the development of the diving helmet, he rejected it saying that it had no foundation.[17] Charles received £400, a considerable sum which would have been sufficient to secure a better standard of living for him.

This windfall undoubtedly raised his spirits, at least temporarily. In 1845 he remarried, this time to Mary Bond, a widow of 38 years of age. He used his money to continue in a futile search for his next winning invention. The previous year he had been granted a provisional patent[18] for improvements in constructing, propelling, and steering vessels. No specification was enrolled, but the *Hampshire Telegraph*,[19] reporting the salvage operations on the *Lady Charlotte*, mentions his ideas for using compressed air to steer ships and to drive carriages through tunnels. In March 1847 he tried to attract the interest of the Admiralty in a new type of gun in a 'plan to better fortify the coast',[20] involving a method of mounting guns on revolving railways in circular batteries. In April, he was back at the Admiralty with a model for a 90-gun ship.[21] It all came to nothing.

Charles must have been suffering from great anxiety and depression. He was said to have been in constant fear of being confined in a lunatic asylum again. He and his wife were living in modest rooms at 5 Providence Place, Limehouse. Early in the morning of 7 November 1848, whilst still in bed, he raised a razor to his throat and made a purposeful incision, completely severing the major veins and arteries. He closed the razor, and died.[22] He was fifty-two. Two days later an inquest was held in the Lord Hood Tavern, in Rich Street, near his home. Charles's body was on view. The coroner's verdict was that he had taken his life whilst temporarily insane. His place of burial has never been found.

Charles Deane was a tragic character. Sadly, his mental instability was to prove his ultimate downfall. However, his legacy to the world of diving is inestimable, and his contribution, together with that of his younger brother John, to the birth of the diving industry deserves to be more highly acknowledged.

John Deane went on to become the country's foremost 'submarine engineer'.[23] He worked directly for most of the major civil engineers of his day, and was hired by the Admiralty as their principal submarine engineer in the Crimea for most of the Crimean War. John's diving career spanned twenty-eight years compared to Charles's eight. In 1836[24] he had a small manual for the diving apparatus printed in Gosport, entitled *Method of using Deane's patent diving apparatus*. He retired to Ramsgate in 1856 where he lived a further twenty-eight years in a close and religious family. He died in 1884, and is buried in a modest grave in Ramsgate cemetery.

17. Public Record Office, WO 47/2010, 3 July 1844.
18. No. 10205, 30 May 1844.
19. 26 November 1838.
20. Public Record Office, WO 44/623, 31 March 1847.
21. Public Record Office, ADM 12/477, 959.10, Pro D 153, 17 April 1847.
22. *Morning Chronicle*, London, 10 November 1848.
23. A title he gave himself.
24. The manual is undated, but circumstantial evidence enables it to be dated to 1836.

5.   The handbill printed to publicise the Exhibition (courtesy, Nigel Phillips).

THE BOOK

Charles Deane published *Submarine Researches* partly in an attempt to estab-lish his credentials as *the* inventor of the 'improved diving apparatus', and as *the* leading proponent of its use. On the lithographed title he promotes himself as the inventor of the apparatus, but in truth his brother John was not only the co-inventor, but an even greater proponent of its use, something Charles never acknowledged. It is noteworthy that he never mentions John once in his book, nor indeed anyone else who assisted him. Charles has perhaps inadvert-ently given some credit to his brother in Plate 1, where Charles is seen working on the wreck of the *Royal George* on 30 October 1834. The supporting vessel, which has the name *Mary of Ramsgate* clearly depicted on its transom, belonged to John Deane and William Edwards, who were then using her as a full time diving support vessel (there is no evidence that Charles ever owned or operated his own vessel).

In the six years that had passed since their first commercial dive (on the wreck of the *Carn Brea Castle* in 1829[25]), until the publication of *Submarine Researches* in 1835, the two brothers had proved that their diving apparatus was a simple, reliable, effective, and safe system of working under water. One of the reasons for publishing *Submarine Researches* was to publicise the versatility of the equipment, including its applications in marine civil engineering (in docks and harbours, and on bridge foundations), and in the salvage of vessels and valuable cargoes.

But Charles's principal purpose in publishing the book was undoubtedly to promote his acclaimed 'Submarine Exhibition' at 209 Regent Street, London, in July 1835 (figure 5). The main exhibits consisted of items raised from the wreck of the *Royal George*, including a 'brass'[26] 24-pounder cannon, weighing two and a half tons. The *Royal George* material was collected mainly by John Deane (together with his partner from Whitstable, William Edwards) who was diving almost continuously on the wreck during the years 1834–1836. Before the salvaged artefacts appeared at the Regent Street Exhibition in London, the cannon and an 'iron and copper pot . . . with bones, which must have been stewing at the time of the ship's sinking' had been placed on temporary display by John Deane at the Castle Tavern in Gosport.[27]

The text

The book is a simple collection of separate items, brought together, possibly in a hurry, to produce a usable marketing document. No effort was made to link the various sections together. Nevertheless, the book provides a unique insight into the first seven years of the diving industry.

Notably the first section of text concerns the wreck of HMS *Royal George* at Spithead. This was the highest profile and historically most significant diving project in which Charles Deane was ever involved. His successful dive on the wreck in 1832 established a landmark in diving history. By the time Charles had published this monograph in 1835, he and his brother had salvaged many bronze cannon from the wreck, and they were planning to use explosives to open it up and gain access to the wealth of valuable material inside. Had Charles not been thwarted in his plans by Colonel Pasley, he might have made his fame and fortune.

Following a brief introduction to the background of the sinking (pages 3–4), presumably written by Charles Deane, first-hand accounts are given by two survivors of the wreck, Charles Blundy, then aged seventy five (pages 4–6), and Mr Ingram (pages 7–18), which was copied from an account in the *Penny Magazine*. The main part of the text of the book (pages 14–23) comprises 'Extracts from Mr. Deane's Journal' (evidently Charles's private journal, now lost),

25. 'Under the Sea', in *Cornhill Magazine*, Vol. 17, Jan.–June 1868, p. 673.
26. The cannon is said here to be made of brass, but it was actually bronze.
27. *Hampshire Telegraph*, 8 June 1835.

which consists of legends to accompany the 19 plates, giving historically important information such as dates, depths of water, background to the diving operations, etc. Finally, two short items are included. The first is a 'certificate' presented to Charles Deane by an agent for Lloyd's underwriters for his work in salvaging the sloop *Endeavour* together with its valuable cargo of copper. The second is an extract from a report by Messrs. Walker and Burges, civil engineers, commending the use of the diving equipment at Blackfriars Bridge. Both of these projects feature in the plates which follow.

The illustrations

The Exhibition at 209 Regent Street featured a unique display of 'a number of valuable and curious Relics which he has recently saved from the Wrecks of His Majesty's Ships and East Indiamen; and also 20 Oil Paintings by MEADOWS, covering nearly 1400 square feet of Canvass, illustrative of the various ways in which the Apparatus has been so successfully employed'.[28]

The oil paintings are of special significance, but sadly they no longer exist. The artist was almost certainly James Meadows (1798–1864), who produced the twenty paintings for the Exhibition, and nineteen are reproduced in *Submarine Researches*. The legends for the paintings, or 'Descriptions of the Views of Mr. Deane's Operations with the Diving Apparatus, now on exhibition at 209, Regent Street' (p. 14 of the 1835 issue) comprise the bulk of the text of the book. It seems likely that the plates in the book are based directly on Meadows' paintings, but the plates are unsigned (except by the printer, Hullmandel) and no acknowledgement is given to the artist. On the other hand, as the drawings exhibit a high degree of correctness of scale and authenticity of detail, both above and below water, it is evident that Charles Deane had a very close involvement in their production, ensuring that they provided an accurate representation of his operations. They might even be his own work. Meadows' large oil paintings may then have been based on these drawings, and not *vice versa*. Be that as it may, very few illustrations exist of the original Deane diving helmet and dress, and for that reason the drawings in *Submarine Researches* are of very great importance. Frustratingly, complete detail is missing, but sufficient detail is shown to permit the general arrangement to be made out.

The edge of the skirt round the bottom of the corselet appears in many of the plates. One piece of equipment which cannot be seen, though, is the waterproof 'Macintosh' suit, as it is covered by the protective canvas jacket and trousers. The air pipe is seen looped under the diver's left arm before going up to the surface, and both the life-line and the air pipe are seen being tended at the surface. A code of signals was established so that, by a predetermined series of pulls on either the life-line or the air pipe, signals could be passed between the diver and the tenders. The tenders always held their lines carefully so that they could feel the movements of the diver. They also had to ensure that just the right amount of tension was kept on the lines to allow the diver freedom to move, but not so little that loose coils could entangle or trap him. The tender holding Charles's signal line in Plate 2 is depicted as a young lad, and is in fact

---

28. The handbill; 1400 square feet of canvas comprises twenty paintings each 10 feet by 7 feet (for example), a considerable display.

Charles Deane junior, who would have been seventeen years of age in 1835. He was then described as 'of slender figure, and apparently of weak constitution. . .'.[29] As soon as he was old enough, he became his father's diving tender; it was reported in 1832 that 'a small rope is tied round his [Charles Deane's] middle, the end of which is held on board by his son, a fine lad of about twelve years of age, the only person whom his father even permits to touch this important part of the apparatus.'[30]

The diving operations selected for inclusion in the book represent a cross-section of the commercial applications of helmet diving in which Charles Deane was involved. These included civil engineering work in docks and on bridge foundations, as well as the salvage of entire vessels or their valuable cargoes. However the book does not cover all of his diving operations during this period. Notable amongst the exclusions are two highly successful treasure diving projects in Ireland. One of these was in 1833–1834 on the wreck of the slave ship *Enterprise*, which sank off the Copeland Islands, near Belfast, and the other was the *Lady Charlotte* (for Lloyd's), in southern Ireland. Both Charles and John Deane made a considerable amount of money from these two wrecks.

PLATE 1 (the *Royal George*, off Portsmouth)

This plate shows Charles working on the main deck in October 1834. Interesting details include the use of a block and tackle to suspend the rope ladder, the three-point mooring of the *Mary* to ensure that it remained constantly in position over the wreck while the diver was down, and the separate tenders for the diver's lifeline and air hose. The wreck is shown correctly listing to port.

PLATE 2 (the *Carn Brea Castle*, south coast of the Isle of Wight)

This is an important drawing because it represents the first commercial application of the Deane diving equipment, in 1829. However Charles has used a little artistic licence here because contemporary accounts described the air pump as a forge bellows and the helmet as a leather prototype with only two windows. It was not until the following year that the Deanes could afford to buy a force pump (as depicted).

The attention to detail in the drawing of the figures is fascinating. We know that Charles's life-line was tended by his son, and the drawing appears to show a young man. The other figures appear as if they were intended to depict actual individuals. For example, the representation of the man tending the diver's air hose would fit John Deane very well, who was twenty-nine years of age at the time and of stocky build. It would certainly be logical for him to be tending the air hose.

It was important for Charles to show that the diver could use his hands at sea bed level, for the open helmet might have been criticised for being unable to permit the user to reach that low without losing the air from the helmet as it tilted forward. It is interesting that the diver is holding his head and helmet fairly upright whilst working at the bottom.

Further interesting details include the weights attached to the bottom of the wooden ladder to hold it down, the distance line secured to the bottom of

29. *The Times*, 1 October 1839.   30. *Arcana of Science*, 1833, pp. 83–84.

18

the ladder which allowed the diver to return to the ladder in the poor or even zero visibility, and the buoyant rum barrels trapped against the deck-head.

PLATES 3 & 4 (the *Boyne*, off Southsea beach)

These again appear as authentic representations. The rather shallow depth is correct. Tying off the marker buoy line on the rudder pintle would be reasonable (Plate 3). The use of a long wooden ladder, rather than a rope ladder, fits with contemporary accounts of the Deanes' experimenting with a sectional ladder invented by Captain Manby (who became famous for his invention of a shipwreck rescue apparatus fired from a mortar). They later abandoned Manby's ladder because it would have given serious problems when being handled from a surface vessel lurching up and down on the waves. The three-point mooring of the surface vessel is again depicted.

PLATES 5, 6 & 7
(Stangate Creek, at the entrance to the River Medway, near Chatham, Kent)

These drawings depict three different diving jobs for the Admiralty, all of which involved clearing fouled anchors. The depths of 30, 54 and 27 feet are accurately reproduced, as is the naval launch. Being a sheltered location, it appears that the surface vessels were adequately moored fore and aft. As the Admiralty was potentially a major customer, the Deanes would have been very keen to introduce their services to them at every opportunity.

PLATES 8, 9 & 10 (the London docks)

There was a huge amount of potential work in the many docks up and down the Thames, so Charles Deane has chosen to illustrate typical dock-work in these three plates. Note in Plate 8 the physiques of the tenders on the signal line and the air hose – they once again fit the known characteristics of the slender Charles Deane junior and the stocky John Deane respectively.

PLATE 11 (Blackfriars Bridge, London)

The work on the foundations of Blackfriars Bridge in the Thames in 1832 marked the first application of the diving helmet to civil engineering. It is of special relevance that this work was carried out for the eminent civil engineering partnership Messrs. Walker and Burges. Mr. Walker himself also carried out some dives with the same equipment and became a great proponent of its use. The exercise was so successful that Charles Deane was invited to present a paper to the Institution of Civil Engineers the following year.

PLATES 12 to 19
(the sloop *Endeavour*, on the west coast of Kintyre, western Scotland)

These plates illustrate the successful salvage in 1833 of the cargo and hull of the sloop *Endeavour*, which represents the first application of the diving helmet to that type of work. The operation was brilliantly conducted and it is described in detail in the legends. The text also refers to Charles Deane taking with him a lad of about fifteen to attend to his signals – Charles Deane junior would have been fifteen years old that year.

SUBMARINE RESEARCHES

ON

THE WRECKS OF HIS MAJESTY'S LATE SHIPS

ROYAL GEORGE, BOYNE,

AND OTHERS,

BY

Mr. C. A. DEANE,

IN HIS IMPROVED DIVING APPARATUS;

WITH

AN INTRODUCTORY ACCOUNT OF THE LOSS OF THE
ROYAL GEORGE,

BY TWO OF HER SEAMEN,

WHO ARE YET SURVIVORS OF THAT AWFUL CATASTROPHE.

EXHIBITION, 209, REGENT STREET.

LONDON:

PRINTED BY J. DAVY, QUEEN STREET, SEVEN DIALS.

1835.

PRICE THREE SHILLINGS.

6.　The title-page of the 1835 issue.

BIBLIOGRAPHY

Collation: 12 leaves, lithographed title, and 19 lithographed plates on 18 sheets.

Contents: lithographed title, with a fanciful illustration of an underwater scene depicting various items of a shipwreck including a cannon, an anchor and a capstan, and a brief quotation from Shakespeare; letterpress title ('Submarine Researches. . .'); text pages numbered (3)–24; and 19 numbered plates (the last two are half-page on the same sheet).

There was only one edition, known in two issues: the first is dated 1835 (figure 6), and has references to Deane's Exhibition at 209 Regent Street on the title and on p. 14, and on the verso of the title where it states that his diving apparatus was also on view at the Exhibition. The second issue is dated 1836, and omits the references to the Exhibition. The price was also increased from sixpence to three shillings. It was issued in blue wrappers, with the title 'Deane's Submarine Researches' within a typographical border on the upper wrapper. It is the second issue which is reproduced here in facsimile.

Six copies have so far been located: the British Library, London (formerly in the Patent Office library), the Institution of Civil Engineers (London), two copies in the New York Public Library, and two in private collections. The copy in the British Library and one of those in the New York Public Library are of the first issue, the others are second issue. The British Library copy has the signature of William Elliot Henslow on the front endpaper. The copy of the first issue in the New York Public Library has a letter from Charles Deane (dated 13 July 1835, and signed 'C. A. Deane') to the editor of an unnamed journal enclosing an invitation to the Exhibition, and the copy of the book; the second issue is inscribed by the eccentric Irish politician Thomas Steele (Daniel O'Connell's 'Head Pacificator of Ireland'). In both copies the plates are missing. The copy in the Institution of Civil Engineers was donated by Thomas Steele in 1838. Steele, an associate member of the Institution, was friendly with both of the Deane brothers, and he had been allowed the privilege of diving in their equipment, once in Ireland and once on the wreck of the *Mary Rose* off Portsmouth.

ACKNOWLEDGEMENTS

Michael Fardell; Nigel Phillips; Carol Morgan of the Institution of Civil Engineers, London; and Barbara Berliner of the New York Public Library.

DEANE'S

SUBMARINE RESEARCHES

Sketches under
THE SEA:
OR
Illustrations of Diving Operations,
performed by
C. A. DEANE,
the Inventor

Printed by C. Hullmandel.

Methought I saw a thousand fearful wrecks;

*　　*　　*　　*

Wedges of gold, great Anchors heaps of pearl,
Inestimable stones, unvalued jewels
All scatter'd in the bottom of the Sea

Shakespeare

SUBMARINE RESEARCHES

ON

THE WRECKS OF HIS MAJESTY'S LATE SHIPS

ROYAL GEORGE, BOYNE,

AND OTHERS,

BY

Mr. C. A. DEANE,

IN HIS IMPROVED DIVING APPARATUS;

WITH

AN INTRODUCTORY ACCOUNT OF THE LOSS OF THE
ROYAL GEORGE,

BY TWO OF HER SEAMEN,

WHO ARE YET SURVIVORS OF THAT AWFUL CATASTROPHE.

LONDON:

PRINTED AND SOLD BY J. DAVY, QUEEN STREET, SEVEN DIALS.

1836.

PRICE THREE SHILLINGS.

LOSS OF THE ROYAL GEORGE

OF ONE HUNDRED GUNS,

AT SPITHEAD,

ON THE 29TH OF AUGUST, 1782.

———◆———

THE loss of the Royal George, at her anchorage at Spithead, in 1782, was one of those fatal events which tended to cast a temporary gloom over the brilliant career of the British Navy,—an event which deprived England of a highly gifted admiral, and nearly all the officers and crew of his ship, amounting, with the women who were on board, to about nine hundred souls.

Several* attempts, sanctioned by government, have been made to raise her, but owing to various causes, the principal of which perhaps was the size and weight of the ship, all have failed; and it was not until Mr. Deane's operations, with his more complete diving apparatus, took place, that any thing of much value was recovered from her. Equipped in his submarine dress, Mr. Deane has successfully invaded the realms of the ocean, and has descended to the wreck of this once noble ship, in her oozy bed, by means of a common rope ladder, and penetrating the hidden and slimy walks of her once fair decks, amidst the oaken tombs of her brave crew, has recovered, at various times, several brass guns of considerable value.

Time has left few in the present day of those who were saved from the ship, but her seventh lieutenant, (aid de camp of Admiral Kempenfeldt, the present Admiral Sir Philip Henderson Durham,

---

* See Nautical Magazine, vol. i. p. 592, for an account of these attempts; and p. 359 of the same volume, for some notice of Mr. Deane's proceedings on the Boyne.

G.C.B.) the only officer alive who then belonged to her, has kindly presented us with the following anecdote, more immediately relating to himself.

When the Royal George was going down, Lieutenant Durham threw off his coat and dashed into the water, where he was seized by a drowning marine, by whom he was twice carried down. On rising the second time, Lieutenant Durham succeeded in extricating himself from the dying man's grasp, by tearing off his waistcoat, and he, with one of the seamen, was eventually saved by seizing the halyards from the mizen topmast head, by which they reached the mast head, from whence they were taken with great difficulty by a boat. The poor marine's body was washed on shore a fortnight afterwards, with the waistcoat, by which he had caught hold of Lieutenant Durham, so firmly twisted round his arm, that a pencil case, bearing the lieutenant's initials, was found safe in the pocket, and restored to the owner. The Captain, under whose direction, with that of first Lieutenant Saunders, the ship was careening, was on the quarter deck at the time the accident occurred, and ran down to warn the Admiral, who was in his cabin; but he was unable to effect his purpose, from the cabin door having become fixed. When Lieutenant Durham had reached a place of temporary security, he observed the Captain holding by the weather mizen top sail-yard-arm, and sent a boat to his aid. These two were the only officers saved. The number of the ship's company on board was nearly 800.

One of the Seamen who belonged to the Royal George, and who was among the few persons saved, relates the melancholy event in the following words :—

I joined the Royal George, of one hundred guns, at Spithead, in December, 1779, being then nineteen years of age, having been drafted from the Princess Amelia, three-decker, and guard ship at Spithead. Lord Rodney was there, in the Sandwich, and Admiral Digby, in the Prince George; on board the latter ship was Prince William Henry, our present gracious King.

In January, 1782, the Royal George was docked at Plymouth, and joined the grand fleet at Spithead, where she changed officers: Admiral Kempenfeldt, Captain Waghorn, and First Lieutenant Saunders, joining her.

She left Spithead with the grand fleet, and cruised in the channel; but returned to Spithead again, being leaky. The leak was found to arise from the pipe leading through the ship's bottom to a cistern in the well from which the water was pumped for washing decks. To get at the leak, at 5 o'clock on the morning of the 29th of August, 1782, all hammocks were piped up, and the word passed for stowing them on the larboard side on the booms. When this was done, the drummer was called to beat all hands to quarters;—I ran to mine, which was the sixth gun on the main-deck. The order was given to run over to leeward all the main-deck and also the quarter-deck and forecastle guns. The middle and lower-deck guns were run in on the weather side, as far as the breechings would allow; and on the lee side, both middle and lower deck, the guns were run out—the lower-deck ports consequently being open, occasioned the ship to fill and sink.

When this happened, I was stationed on the middle-gun-deck, at the tackle fall, hoisting provisions out of the after-hold, and rolling the same to leeward, to give the ship more heel, to enable the carpenters to get at the leak on the weather side. This work continued until about half-past 8, when the water was at intervals dashing in at the lower-deck ports;—at this moment, the captain was standing at the entering port on the middle-gun-deck. About ten minutes after this the danger was discovered, as the water began more rapidly to dash in at the lower-deck ports. The drummer was immediately called to beat to quarters; when I left the tackle fall where I was stationed, and run upon the main-deck to my gun, the sixth. When I got there, four of us, Joseph Woodcock (the captain of the gun), myself, and two others, immediately hooked the tackles on to windward, and while in the act of endeavouring to bouse our gun to windward, I saw the signal lieutenant (the present Admiral Sir Philip Henderson Durham) on the weather gangway, hailing with a speaking trumpet, "Bouse, bouse away, the ship is sinking!"—the words were scarcely out of his mouth when the ship capsized. At this moment, being obliged for our own safety to drop the ends of the falls, the gun running away to leeward, I scrambled up to windward by the assistance of the tackle fall, and got out of the weather port; as also did my old companion, Joseph Woodcock, who died about six years ago, in the Royal Hospital at Greenwich,—whom I, with Charles Wilson, and several other old shipmates, saved from the wreck of the Royal George, used to meet particularly to commemorate the 29th of August, which we considered our birth-day. They are all dead; and I am now left to myself to reflect on my miraculous escape.

I must now go back to getting out of the port. Not being able to swim, I stood there until she filled. There were about three hundred of us poor fellows standing on the ship's bottom, singing out "Boats, boats, for God's sake!" The suction of the ship made a horrible noise; when down we went altogether, clinging hold of each other, many catching hold of me, and I catching hold of others; and after going down several times, on coming up, the rest of my unfortunate companions were pretty clear of me. In the confusion in the water, I caught hold of a drum, and being nearly exhausted got my head entangled underneath it. Something at that moment scratched my head, it proved to be a pig swimming about, and I clung to his neck for a short time; when, providentially, up floated some of the hammocks, and I let go my hold of the pig for a hammock.

By this time, the ship had filled, sunk, and righted, part of the rigging remaining above water;—when one of my shipmates hallowed out "Charley, Charley, strike off here!" I let go my hold of the hammock, and did so; never having swam either before or since, I then got on the rigging, much exhausted, and where I recollect seeing many more of the ship's company come up and swim to the rigging also. There was, I suppose, about one hundred and fifty of us, and one woman, with her husband, whose name was John Horn, and who was carried on board the Victory with me. It is supposed that about six hundred men, with unfortunate Admiral Kempenfeldt, and three hundred women, here perished.

CHARLES BLUNDY, aged seventy-five,
late Ordinary Seaman of the Royal George,
and now living at 19, Newcastle Street, Bethnal Green.

March 9th, 1835.

Another of the Survivors, Mr. Ingram, a very respectable and intelligent man, who lives, and has lived for many years, at Woodford, a village exactly midway between Gloucester and Bristol—relates as follows, in a recent number of the *Penny Magazine*. We have, however, corrected his narrative in one or two places, on the high authority we have mentioned.

The Royal George was a ship of one hundred guns. Originally her guns had been all brass, but when she was docked at Plymouth, either in the spring of 1782 or the year before, the brass forty-two pounders on her lower gun deck were taken out of her as being too heavy, and iron thirty-two pounders put there in their stead: so that after that she carried brass twenty-four pounders on her main-deck, quarter-deck, and poop, brass thirty-two pounders on her middle-deck, and iron thirty-two pounders on her lower-deck. She did not carry any carronades. She measured sixty-six feet from the kelson to the taffrail; and, being a flag ship, her lanterns were so big, that the men used to go into them to clean them.

In August, 1782, the Royal George had come to Spithead. She was in a very complete state, with hardly any leakage, so that there was no occasion for the pumps to be touched oftener than once in every three or four days. By the 29th of August she had got six months' provision on board, and also many tons of shot. The ship had her top-gallant-yards up, the blue flag of Admiral Kempenfelt was flying at the mizen, and the ensign was hoisted on the ensign-staff,— and she was in about two days to have sailed to join the grand fleet in the Mediterranean. It was ascertained that the water-cock must be taken out and a new one put in. The water-cock is something like the tap of a barrel—it is in the hold of the ship on the starboard side, and at that part of the ship called the well. By turning a thing which is inside the ship, the sea-water is let into a cistern in the hold, and it is from that pumped up to wash the decks. In some ships the water is drawn up the side in buckets, and there is no water-cock. To get out the old water-cock, it was necessary to make the ship heel so much on her larboard side as to raise the outside of this water-cock above water. This was done at about 8 o'clock on the morning of the 29th of August. To do it the whole of the guns on the larboard side were run out as far as they would go, quite to the breasts of the guns, and the starboard guns drawn in a midships and secured by tackles, two to every gun, one on each side the gun. This brought the water nearly on a level with the port-holes of the larboard side of the lower gun-deck. The men were working at this water-cock on the outside of the ship for near an hour, the ship remaining all on one side as I have stated.

At about 9 o'clock A.M., or rather before, we had just finished our breakfast, and the last lighter, with rum on board, had come along-side: this vessel was a sloop of about fifty tons, and belonged to three brothers, who used to carry things on board the men-of-war. She was lashed to the larboard side of the Royal George, and we were piped to clear the lighter and get the rum out of her, and stow it in the hold of the Royal George. I was in the waist of our ship, on the larboard side, bearing the rum-casks over, as some men of the Royal George were aboard the sloop to sling them.

At first no danger was apprehended from the ship being on one side, although the water kept dashing in at the port holes at every wave; and there being mice in the lower part of the ship, which were disturbed by the water which dashed in, they were hunted in the water by the men, and there had been a rare game going on. However, by about 9 o'clock the additional quantity of rum on board the ship, and also the quantity of sea-water which had dashed in through the port-holes, brought the larboard port-holes of the lower gun-deck nearly level with the sea.

As soon as that was the case, the carpenter went on the quarter-deck to the lieutenant of the watch, to ask him to give orders to right ship, as the ship could not bear it. However, the lieutenant made him a very short answer, and the carpenter then went below. This officer was the third lieutenant; he had not joined us long; his name I do not recollect; he was a good-sized man, between thirty and forty years of age. The men called him "Jib-and-Staysail Jack," for, if he had the watch in the night, he would be always bothering the men to alter the sails, and it was "up jib" and "down jib," and "up foresail" and "down foresail," every minute. However, the men considered him more of a troublesome officer than a good one; and, from a habit he had of moving his fingers about when walking the quarter-deck, the men said he was an organ-player from London, but I have no reason to know that that was the case. The captain's name was Waghorn. He was on board, but where he was I do not know;—however, captains, if anything is to be done when the ship is in harbour, seldom interfere, but leave it all to the officer of the watch. The admiral was either in his cabin, or in the steerage, I do not know which; and the barber, who had been to shave him, had just left. The admiral was a man upwards of seventy years of age; he was a thin tall man, who stooped a good deal.

As I have already stated, the carpenter left the quarter-deck and went below. In a very short time he came up again, and asked the lieutenant of the watch to right ship, and said again that the ship could not bear it. Myself and a good many more were at the waist of the ship and at the gangways, and heard what passed, as we knew the danger, and began to feel aggrieved, for there were some capital seamen aboard, who knew what they were about quite as well or better than the officers.

In a very short time, in a minute or two I should think, Lieutenant (now Admiral Sir P. H.) Durham ordered the drummer to be called to beat to right ship. The drummer was called in a moment, and the ship was then just beginning to sink. I jumped off the gangway as soon as the drummer was called. There was no time for him to beat his drum, and I don't know that he even had time to get it. I ran down to my station, and, by the time I had got there, the men were tumbling down the hatchways one over another to get to their stations as quick as possible to right ship. My station was at the third gun from the head of the ship, on the starboard side of the lower gun-deck, close by where the cable passes, indeed it was just abaft the bight of the cable. I said to the second captain of our gun, whose name was Carrell, (for every gun has a first and second captain, though they are only sailors), "Let us try to bouse our gun out without waiting for the drum, as it will help to right ship." We pushed the gun, but it ran back upon us, and we could not start him. The water then rushed in at nearly all the port-holes of the larboard side of the lower gun-deck, and I directly said to Carrell, "Ned, lay hold of the ring-bolt and jump out at the port-hole; the ship is sinking, and we shall be all drowned." He laid hold of the ring-bolt, and jumped out at the port-hole into the sea: I believe he was drowned, for I never saw him afterwards. I immediately got out at the same port-hole, which was the third from the head of the ship on the starboard side of the lower gun-deck, and when I had done so, I saw the port-hole as full of heads as it could cram, all trying to get out. I caught hold of the best bower-anchor, which was just above me, to prevent falling back again into the port-hole, and seized hold of a woman who was trying to get out at that same port-hole,—I dragged her out. The ship was full of Jews, women, and people selling all sorts of things. I threw the woman from me,—and saw all the heads drop back again in at the port-hole, for the ship had got so much on her larboard side, that the starboard port-holes were as upright as if the men had tried to get out of the top of a chimney with nothing for their legs and feet to act upon. I threw the woman from me, and just after that moment the air that was between decks drafted out at the port-holes very swiftly. It was quite a huff of wind, and it blew my hat off, for I had all my clothes on, including my hat. The ship then sunk in a moment. I tried to swim, but I could not swim a morsel, although I plunged as hard as I could both hands and feet. The sinking of the ship drew me down so,—indeed I think I must have gone down within a yard as low as the ship did. When the ship touched the bottom, the water boiled up a great deal, and then I felt that I could swim, and began to rise.

When I was about half way up to the top of the water, I put my right hand on the head of a man that was nearly exhausted. He wore long hair, as many of the men at that time did; he tried to grapple me, and he put his four fingers into my right shoe alongside the outer edge of my foot. I succeeded in kicking my shoe off, and, putting my hand on his shoulder, I shoved him away,—I then rose to the surface of the water.

At the time the ship was sinking, there was a barrel of tar on the starboard side of her deck, and that had rolled to the larboard and staved as the ship went down, and when I rose to the top of the water the tar was floating like fat on the top of a boiler. I got the tar about my hair and face, but I struck it away as well as I could, and when my head came above water I heard the cannon ashore firing for distress. I looked about me, and at the distance of eight or ten yards from me I saw the main topsail halyard block above water;—the water was about thirteen fathoms deep, and at that time the tide was coming in. I swam to the main topsail halyard block, got on it, and sat upon it, and there I rode. The fore, main, and mizen tops were all above water, as were a part of the bowsprit and part of the ensign-staff, with the ensign upon it.

In going down, the main yard of the Royal George caught the boom of the rum-lighter and sunk her, and there is no doubt that this made the Royal George more upright in the water when sunk than she otherwise would have been, as she did not lie much more on her beam ends than small vessels often do when left dry on a bank of mud.

When I got on the main topsail halyard block I saw the admiral's baker in the shrouds of the mizen-top-mast, and directly after that the woman whom I had pulled out of the port-hole came rolling by: I said to the baker, who was an Irishman named Robert Cleary, "Bob, reach out your hand and catch hold of that woman;—that is a woman I pulled out of the port-hole. I dare say she is not dead." He said "I dare say she is dead enough; it is of no use to catch hold of her." I replied, "I dare say she is not dead." He caught hold of the woman and hung her head over one of the ratlins of the mizen shrouds, and there she hung by her chin, which was hitched over the ratlin, but a surf came and knocked her backwards, and away she went rolling over and over. A captain of a frigate which was lying at Spithead came up in a boat as fast as he could. I dashed out my left hand in a direction towards the woman as a sign to him. He saw it, and saw the woman. His men left off rowing, and they pulled the woman aboard their boat and laid her on one of the thwarts. The captain of the frigate called out to me, "My man, I must take care of those that are in more danger than you." I said "I am safely moored now, Sir." There was a seaman named Hibbs hanging by his two hands from the main-stay; his name was Abel Hibbs, but he was called Monny, and as he hung from the main-stay the sea washed over him every now and then as much as a yard deep over his head, and when he saw it coming he roared out: however, he was but a fool for that, for if he had kept himself quiet he would not have wasted his strength, and would have been able to take the chance of holding on so much the longer. The captain of the frigate had his boat rowed to the main-stay, but they got the stay over part of the head of the boat, and were in great danger before they got Hibbs on board. The captain of the frigate then got all the men that were in the different parts of the rigging, including myself and the baker, into his boat and took us on board the Victory, where the doctors recovered the woman, but she was very ill for three or four days. On board the Victory I saw the body of the carpenter, lying on the hearth before the galley fire; some women were trying to recover him, but he was quite dead.

The captain of the Royal George, who could not swim, was picked up and saved by one of our seamen. The lieutenant of the watch, I believe, was drowned. The number of persons who lost their lives I cannot state with any degree of accuracy, because of there being so many Jews, women, and other persons on board who did not belong to the ship. The complement of the ship was nominally 1000 men, but she was not full. Some were ashore, and sixty marines had gone ashore that morning.

The government allowed 5l. each to the seamen who were on board, and not drowned, for the loss of their things. I saw the list, and there were only seventy-five. A vast number of the best of the men were in the hold stowing away the rum-casks: they must all have perished, and so must many of the men who were slinging the casks in the sloop. Two of the three brothers belonging to the sloop perished, and the other was saved. I have no doubt that the men caught hold of each other, forty or fifty together, and drowned one another—those who could not swim catching hold of those who could; and there is also little doubt that as many got into the launch as could cram into her, hoping to save themselves in that way, and went down in her altogether.

In a few days after the Royal George sunk, bodies would come up, thirty or forty nearly at a time. A body would rise, and come up so suddenly as to frighten any one. The watermen, there is no doubt, made a good thing of it: they took from the bodies of the men their buckles, money, and watches, and then made fast a rope to their heels and towed them to land.

The water-cock ought to have been put to rights before the immense quantity of shot was put on board; but if the lieutenant of the watch had given the order to right ship a couple of minutes earlier, when the carpenter first spoke to him, nothing amiss would have happened; as three or four men at each tackle of the starboard guns would very soon have boused the guns all out, and have righted the ship. At the time this happened, the Royal George was anchored by two anchors from the head. The wind was rather from the north-west,—not much of it,—only a bit of a breeze; and there was no sudden gust or puff of wind which made her heel just before she sunk; it was the weight of metal and the water which had dashed in through the port-holes which sunk her, and not the effect of the wind upon her. Indeed I do not recollect that she had even what is called a stitch of canvass, to keep her head steady as she lay at anchor.

I am now seventy-five years of age, and was about twenty-four when this happened.

DESCRIPTIONS OF THE VIEWS

OF

MR. DEANE'S OPERATIONS

WITH

THE DIVING APPARATUS,

Extracts from Mr. Deane's Journal.

VIEW N.º I.

THE Stern and aftermost part of the ROYAL GEORGE, shew-
ing the condition in which she was found by Mr. Deane.

Oct. 30th, 1834. Equipped in the diving dress; descended by the
ladder from the Mary, in seventy-two feet depth of water, to the
wreck of the Royal George. Found much rubbish, old rope, pieces
of iron, shot, &c. lying about. Succeeded in slinging and sending
up one of the brass guns, a twenty-four pounder.

[By the same means have been recovered, twenty-three of her guns,
namely, fifteen brass twenty-four pounders, formerly belonging to the
middle deck; three brass twelve pounders from the main deck, and
five thirty-two pounders iron lower deckers. They were all found
loaded, the shots and wads being in an excellent state of preservation.]

VIEW N.º II.
THE CARNBREA CASTLE.

August 1829.—Engaged at the back of the Isle of Wight, in
about four fathoms water, sending up part of the cargo of the sunken
East India ship, Carnbrea Castle, for the underwriters at Lloyd's, by

a ladder down the main hatchway. The property consisting of pig lead, tiles, and ingots of copper, &c. Some casks of rum are shewn washed up under the deck above.

This ship struck on a rock, and filled with water, a few weeks sitting upright. At high water the tide was nearly up to the upper deck beams. She is represented as seen at low water, the level of it just below the lower deck. However, a gale of wind coming on, she soon beat to pieces, and breaking her off at the floor heads, her sides, with all moveables, were soon washed on shore; after which, a great part of the remaining cargo was recovered.

VIEW Nº III.

STERN OF THE BOYNE.

Sending up a basket of wine from the wreck in about 27 feet depth of water, in August 1832. His Majesty's ship Boyne, of ninety-eight guns, was ordered by letter from the Navy Board, dated February 3rd, 1795, to have her defects made good at Spithead, and to be stored for channel service. The same letter contained a similar order respecting the Boston. We mention this circumstance, as it was the last occasion on which she was repaired and restowed.

On the 1st of May, in the afternoon, the Boyne while at anchor at Spithead, was observed to be on fire. Signals were immediately made for the fleet, then at Spithead, to get instantly under way, and to render all possible assistance to her crew; all of whom were happily rescued from the fate that seemed to threaten them, by the combined exertions of the officers and crews of the various ships at Spithead.

The weather was beautifully serene, and had it not been for the melancholy accident which caused the fleet to weigh anchor, it would have been regarded as one of the most magnificent scenes that was ever witnessed at Spithead. The fire soon reached the cables of the Boyne, and these being consumed, she floated adrift with the tide then running to the eastward, and the fleet had some difficulty occasionally to keep clear of her. The novelty and grandeur attracted together an immense number of spectators in every place where a view could be obtained; but the curiosity which was at first universally evinced, was somewhat cooled, when it was found that the guns which the Boyne fired from her lower deck were shotted, as was customary during the war, the Boyne being under orders to sail the next day. The consequence was, several shots fell on Southsea beach, to the great alarm and discomfiture of those who had been attracted to the spot; but considering all the lower deckers were shotted, it is remarkable that so little damage was done: the worst accident on record was, the death of three men on board the Queen Charlotte, of one hundred guns, who were killed with shots from the Boyne. Several shots fell near Southsea Castle; and it was nearly opposite this castle that the relics of this magnificent ship, after the explosion of her magazine, sunk on the evening of the 1st of May, 1795.—*Portsmouth Herald*.

VIEW N.º IV.
PART OF THE BOYNE.

August 1832.—Sending up one of the twenty-four pounder guns of the Boyne, from which ship a variety of different articles, such as copper bolts and sheets, shot, pieces of iron of all descriptions were recovered. The articles having the King's mark on them, (a broad arrow), were delivered at his Majesty's Dock-yard, Portsmouth.

VIEW N.º V.
THE SAN FIORENZO'S MOORING CHAIN.

February 28th, 1832.—Employed in Stangate Creek, clearing the moorings of His Majesty's ships, having a launch, and men from His Majesty's ship Imperieuse. Clearing and getting an anchor from the moorings of His Majesty's ship St. Fiorenzo, in 30 feet depth of water.

VIEW No. VI.

IMPERIEUSE'S MOORINGS.

February 1832.—Coming up after bending (tying) a rope to an anchor, linked in the moorings of His Majesty's ship Imperieuse, in Stangate Creek, in 54 feet depth of water. By means of the rope fastened, the lost anchor was recovered.

VIEW No. VII.

THE EVELINE'S ANCHOR.

March 10th, 1832.—Clearing and sending up an anchor of fifteen cwt., to which was attached forty-five fathoms of chain cable, belonging to the ship Eveline, from Alexandria. The anchor had fallen foul in the moorings of His Majesty's ship Christian the 7th, in Stangate Creek, in about 27 feet depth of water.

VIEW No. VIII.

COMMERCIAL DOCK MOORING.

September 1833.—In the act of shackling a chain to one of the old stone moorings in the Commercial Dock, in about three and a half fathoms water, for the Commercial Dock Company.

B

VIEW Nº. IX.

EAST COUNTRY DOCK.

October 1833.—The East Country Dock Company having lost every tide eleven feet of water, owing to the outer main posts not meeting below, Mr. Deane in the act of fitting and nailing a slice piece, which at once remedied the defect.

VIEW Nº. X.

LONDON DOCKS.

November and December 1833.—Employed by the London Dock Company, doing various jobs under water, at the eastern entrance of the London Docks. Represented as employed in twenty-one feet water, clearing obstructions of various kinds from behind the gates.

VIEW Nº. XI.

PIER OF BLACKFRIAR'S BRIDGE.

December 1832.—Employed by Messrs. Walker and Burgess, Civil Engineers, who occasionally made their descents in various depths of water, and from whose reports, with Mr. Deane's, to the City and the House of Commons, the necessary repairs are now taking place. (See Note at page 24.)

VIEW Nº XII.

June 10th, 1833.—The situation of the sloop Endeavour, which struck on a sunken rock in the sound of Gigha, North West Islands of Scotland; afterwards washed off by heavy breakers into 36 feet depth of water.

That the progress of recovering the sloop Endeavour may be distinctly understood, the views of the operations have been arranged in the various stages of their progress. Mr. Deane was sent from London by the wish of Capt. J. Tayler, for the under-writers at Lloyd's: and shipping the machinery for Leith, crossed the country to join a schooner at Campbeltown, in Argyleshire; taking with him his son, a lad about fifteen years of age, to attend to the signals. The skill, activity, and perseverance of Messrs. Watsons, of Campbeltown, and all the men employed, and also their care and attention to Mr. Deane during all his operations under water were most commendable, and contributed in an eminent degree to the success of the undertaking.

---◆---

VIEW Nº XIII.

July 8th.—Employed in the hold of the sunken vessel, in 36 feet depth of water. Commenced, June 10th, 1833, sending up the cargo. A ladder being placed down the main-hatchway; the cargo being sent up the after-hatchway. In first descending, found the hold knee-deep with broken wood, hoops, tiles, bricks, jars; and the staves of several casks of lamp black, all stove by persons endeavouring to grapple up the cargo during the short time the vessel, filled with water, lay on the rock. The circumstance of the lamp black being adrift in the hold, made the operations very difficult at the commencement, as in moving about below made the water so discoloured; all being done, as weather would permit, by feeling only, until at last repeated disturbances washed the hold clear of the black sediment, after the operations of twelve days.

Finding it dangerous and difficult in sending up any more of the cargo, as the sunken vessel began to roll heavily by the least western swell, owing to many tons of dead weight being taken out, resorted to a fresh mode of operations, of removing the vessel to a better spot for working.

VIEW N.º XIV.

In the act of bringing on the purchases to two ends of a chain leading to the schooner above, the bight being round the sunken vessel's windlass for support, the two ends leading through the hawse hole in each bow. The bight of a second chain up the main-hatchway, with a stout spar, through it as a toggle, and then lashed to the deck, and stapled to the chain, the two ends of the chain leading up the after-hatchway. A third chain rove through the rudder trunk, the two ends ready for bringing to for heaving. A great number of empty casks being lashed to the rigging, round the crank and wind-lass, to assist in lifting the vessel. The rudder, in the vessel falling off the rock, became unshipped, and could not be taken out as the vessel lay; consequently, was lashed to the braces, to prevent its slipping down, and taking the ground, in moving the vessel to a more convenient place.

VIEW N.º XV.

The schooner lifting her forward by two treble block purchases, made fast to the chains below and leading to the schooner's bows; a tackle on the hawling part of each fall, forming the purchase, luff upon luff; the slacks of each chain being taken in by fore and aft tackles on the deck. The after part being hove up by the four ends of the chains leading through the after-hatch and rudder trunk. The four chains leading two of each side of the sloop to two stout Spanish windlasses, fitted on balks of timber reaching across the deck, and standing well out from the sides of the vessel. A number of sixteen feet levers being alternately boused down by tackles, which hove up bodily the after part of the sunken vessel. In this position she was warped six miles.

VIEW N.º XVI.

After grounding near the island of Gigha, in about four fathoms water, having no more than four feet flow of tide, shifted the purchase blocks lower down forward, hove all up at high water, and grounded her again in about three and a half fathoms. Commenced unreaving the chains, and sending up the casks. Afterwards, in the usual way of diving, by placing a ladder down the hatchway, finished sending up the remainder of the cargo, consisting of

29 coils of lead pipes, 3 cwt. each
60 bundles of wood hoops
3 boxes of tin, 1 cwt. each
600 tiles
15 jars
9 cases of sheet copper, 7 cwt. each
750 bricks
56 earthen bottles
87 copper bolts, 15 feet long
5 casks of copper nails, 6 cwt. each
89 bars of copper, of various lengths
and 146 sheets of copper, 3 feet square, weighing nearly three tons.

Broke out from abaft the pump, each being necessarily bent in the hold sufficient to come up the after-hatchway. To each separately a small hand vice, attached to the Derrick rope, being screwed on to each sheet, to facilitate the slinging; and for each had to come up the ladder on deck, to bear them clear of the hatchway. After the hold was cleared, with the exception of a few straggling copper bolts, it came on a stiff breeze; when the vessel fell over from the immense weight of her mast, as now represented, with **Mr. Deane** cutting away the lanyards of the shrouds, preparatory to heaving out the mast, which being done with a purchase block, led to the cable of an anchor, carried out for the purpose.

VIEW N.º XVII.

There being only, as before observed, about four feet flow of tide, and having only one vessel to attempt any further operations of lifting, commenced successfully a new mode, in placing under water a sufficient number of empty casks in the hold, under the beams, each cask being lowered from the Derrick, to sink which was a **7 cwt.** case of copper, and further weighted as was necessary to the buoyancy of the cask, thereby allowing the cask, when in the hold, to be placed forward or aft as requisite, with the greatest possible ease ; which by casting off the lanyard attached, the cask rising up under the beams, the case of copper then lying in the hold—which being hove up again in the same manner, sunk a sufficient number, which floated the vessel to the surface: when heaving her a-head at high water, she ebbed so as to enable a sufficient number of empty casks being stapled to the futlin and stauncheons, in such a manner, as to keep the vessel two strakes out of water.

VIEW N.º XVIII.

The Endeavour floated by empty casks in the hold, with her mast, boom, and all her spars lashed on deck, towing from the island of

Gigha round the mull of Cantire, into Campbeltown harbour, about sixty miles, by the Glasgow steam boat, the Duke of Lancaster, Captain Napier.

◆

VIEW N.º XIX.

The Endeavour hawled up, and undergoing repairs in the harbour of Campbeltown, in about fifty-seven days from commencing the operations at the sunken rock in the sound of Gigha.

The following Certificate was presented to Mr. Deane, by the Underwriters of the Endeavour, in acknowledgment of his valuable services on this occasion:

To. MR. C. A. DEANE.

Sir,

At the recommendation of the under-writers of this establishment generally, I beg leave to transmit the following certificate, regarding the important recovery of a cargo, in which they were interested, and had settled the risk on account, considering it a case of total loss. The sloop Endeavour, bound to Leith from Bristol, on her passage by the west of Scotland, intending to make her passage by the Caledonian canal, (being winter), on the 22d of February, 1833, off the west side of the mull of Cantire, struck on a sunken rock, was afterwards washed off by heavy breakers, and sunk in six fathoms water; her cargo, consisting chiefly of copper manufactured, of all descriptions; also a large quantity of lead pipe, bricks, tiles, iron and wood hoops, &c.; which could not be recovered by any other means than diving. I was requested to proceed to the place where the vessel was discovered to be; a small part, about six feet of her mast only above water. I found the ground was good, and every probability of recovering the cargo, although then May, being upwards of three months from the accident happening. I agreed with a party to furnish all means of vessels, with men and the necessary tackle; and on condition of employing Mr. Deane, the attempt was to be made. On my return to London, I found Mr. Deane was disengaged at the time, and agreed with him to proceed to the vessel, with the requisite apparatus; and although the vessel was lying in a very unsafe situation, the whole of the cargo, by his exertions, was recovered, and afterwards the vessel.

The underwriters on the copper, in the above instance, request me to make public this enterprising and effectually beneficial act of Mr. Deane, and consider it worthy of public approbation in a very high degree; and to state, that they benefited to the amount of fifty per cent. on the net proceeds of the property insured, which was all recovered by the exertions of Mr. Deane.

Given under my hand, at Lloyd's, this 12th day of January, 1835.

JAMES TAYLER,
Agent for the Under-writers, Surveyor and Referee.

Extract from Messrs. WALKER and BURGESS's *Report upon Blackfriars' Bridge, dated* 2d *March*, 1833.

" As the common diving bell appeared to us, from its size, to be inconvenient for examining the foundations, without a large excavation near the piers, which it was desirable to avoid, and from its affording the opportunity of examining the vertical face of the stonework, we applied to Mr. Barnard, the Member of Parliament for Greenwich, who has an interest in Deane's patent diving helmet, for the use of that machine. Mr. Deane brought it from Portsmouth, and has attended us during the survey, having, as well as ourselves, frequently descended to the foundations, and examined the work by means of it."

PRINTED BY J. DAVY,
QUEEN STREET, SEVEN DIALS.

Pl. 1.

MARY OF RAMSGATE

Pl. 2.

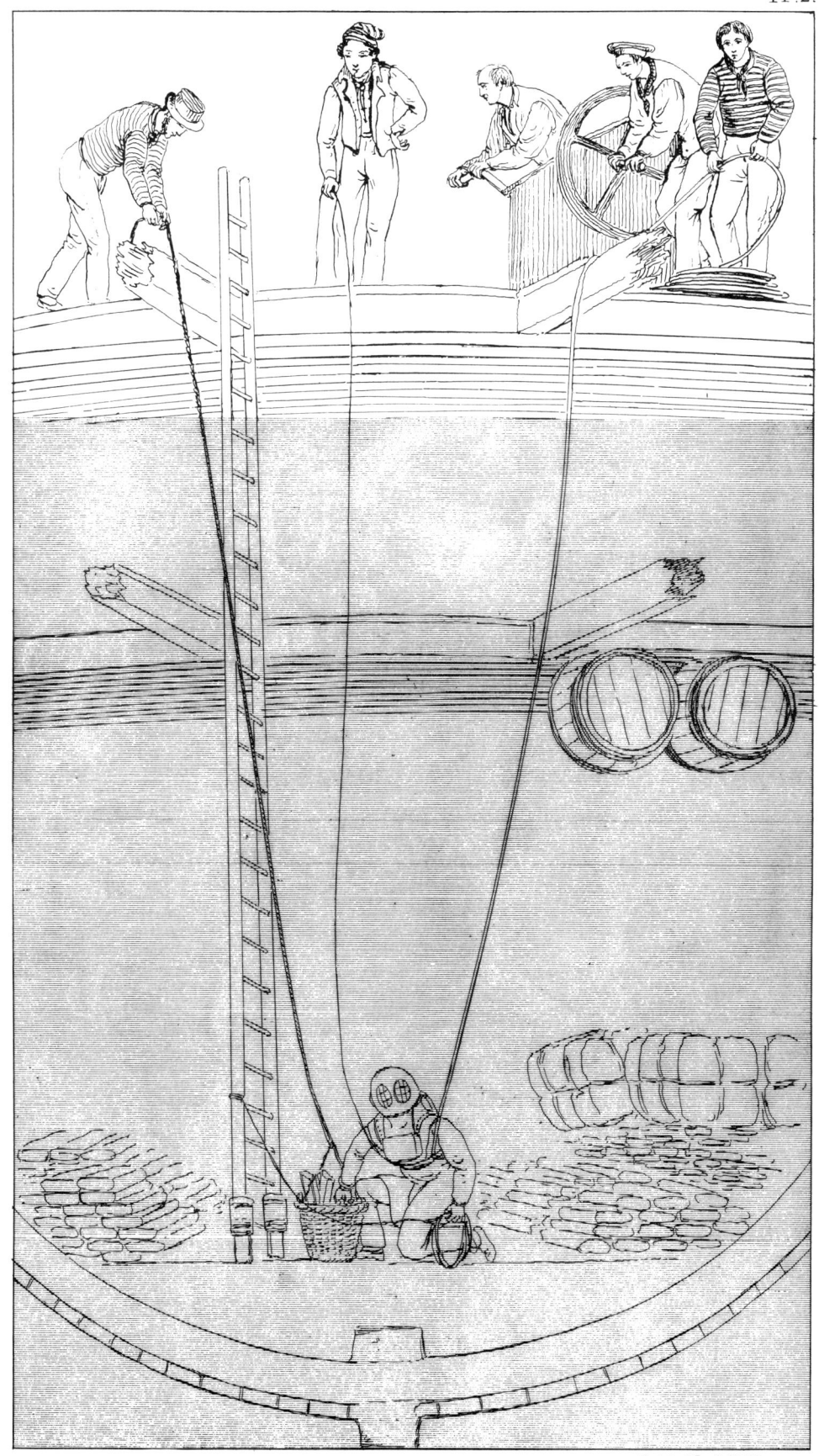

Printed by C. Hullmandel.

Pl. 3.

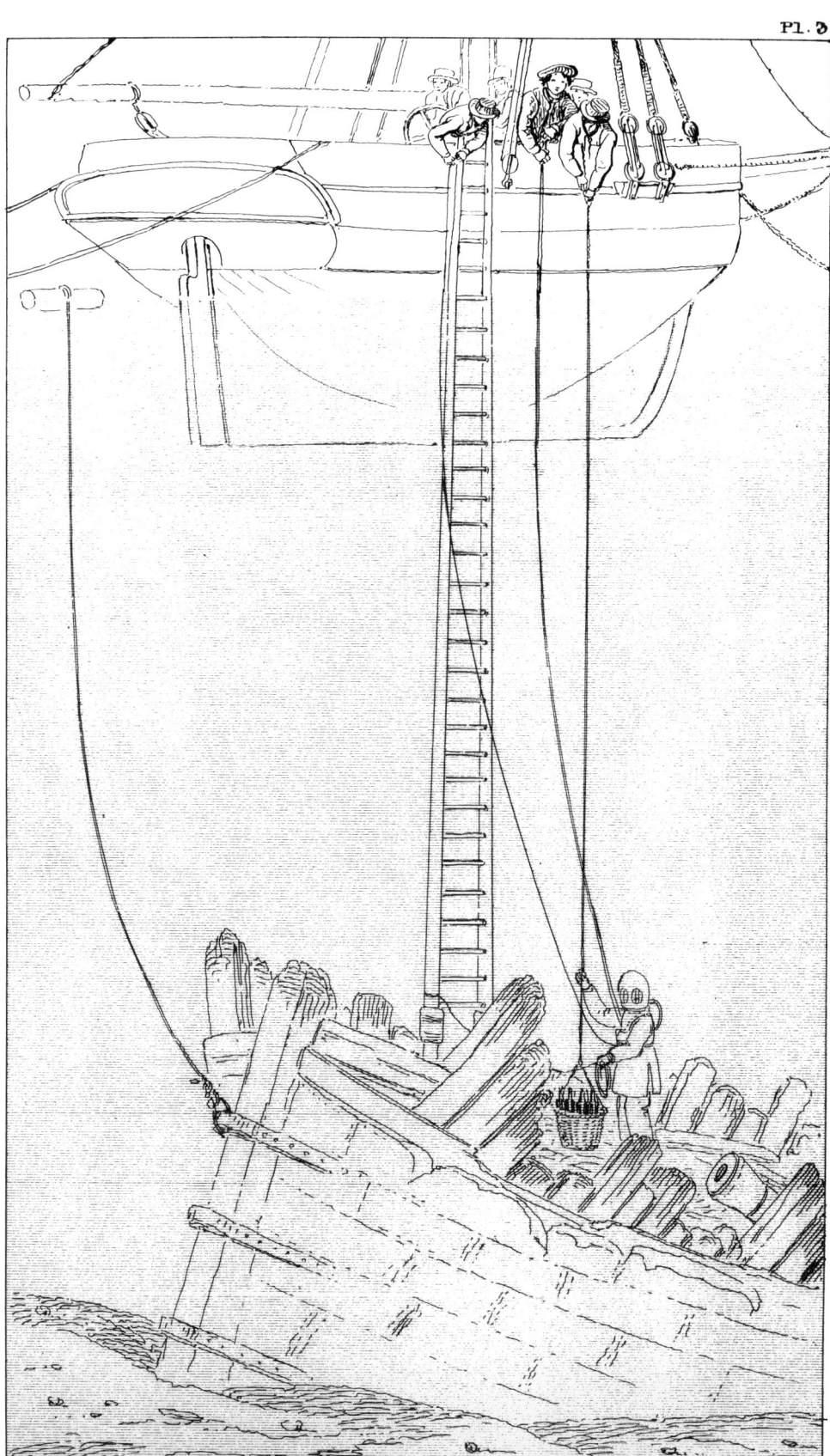

Printed by C. Hullmandel.

Pl. 4.

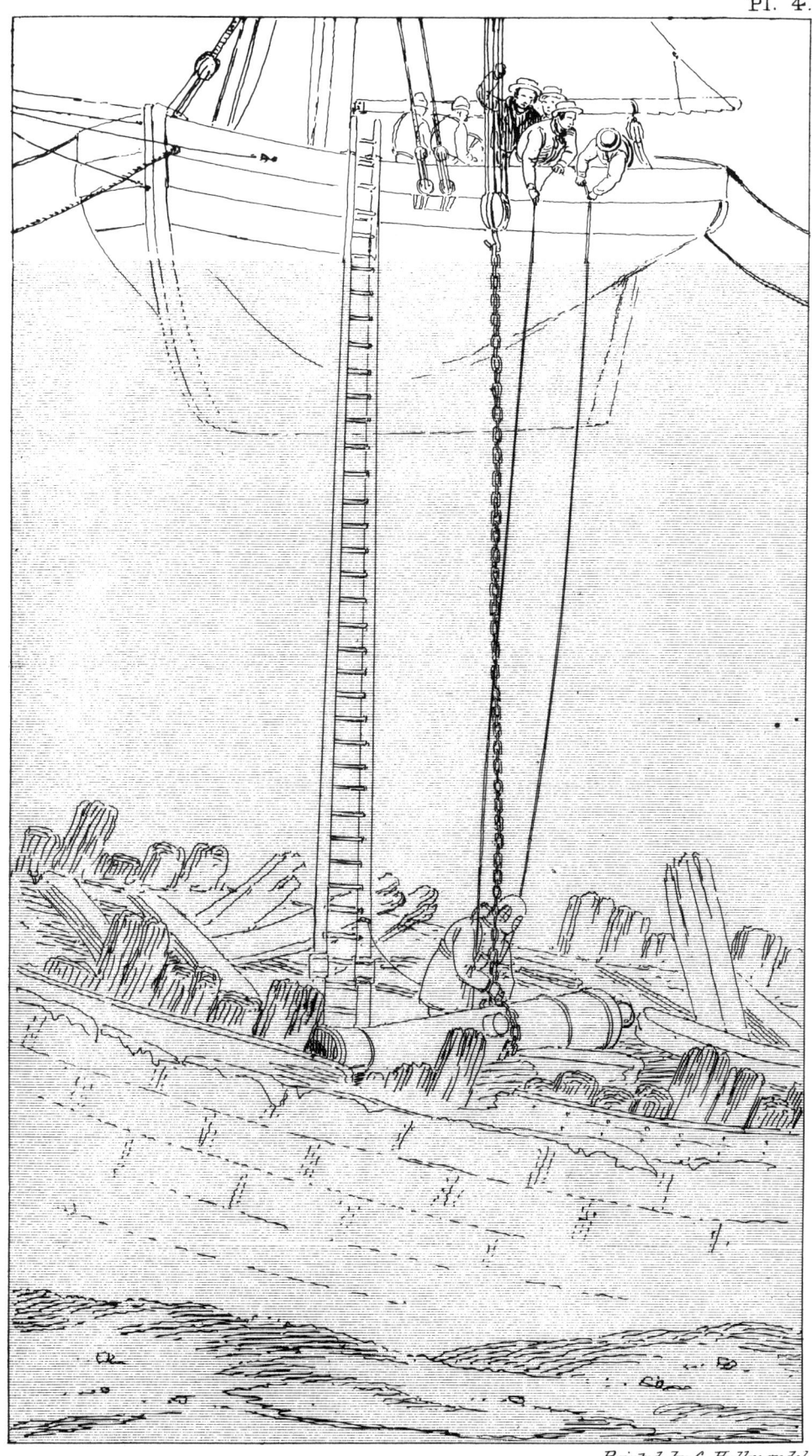

Printed by C. Hullmandel.

Pl. 5.

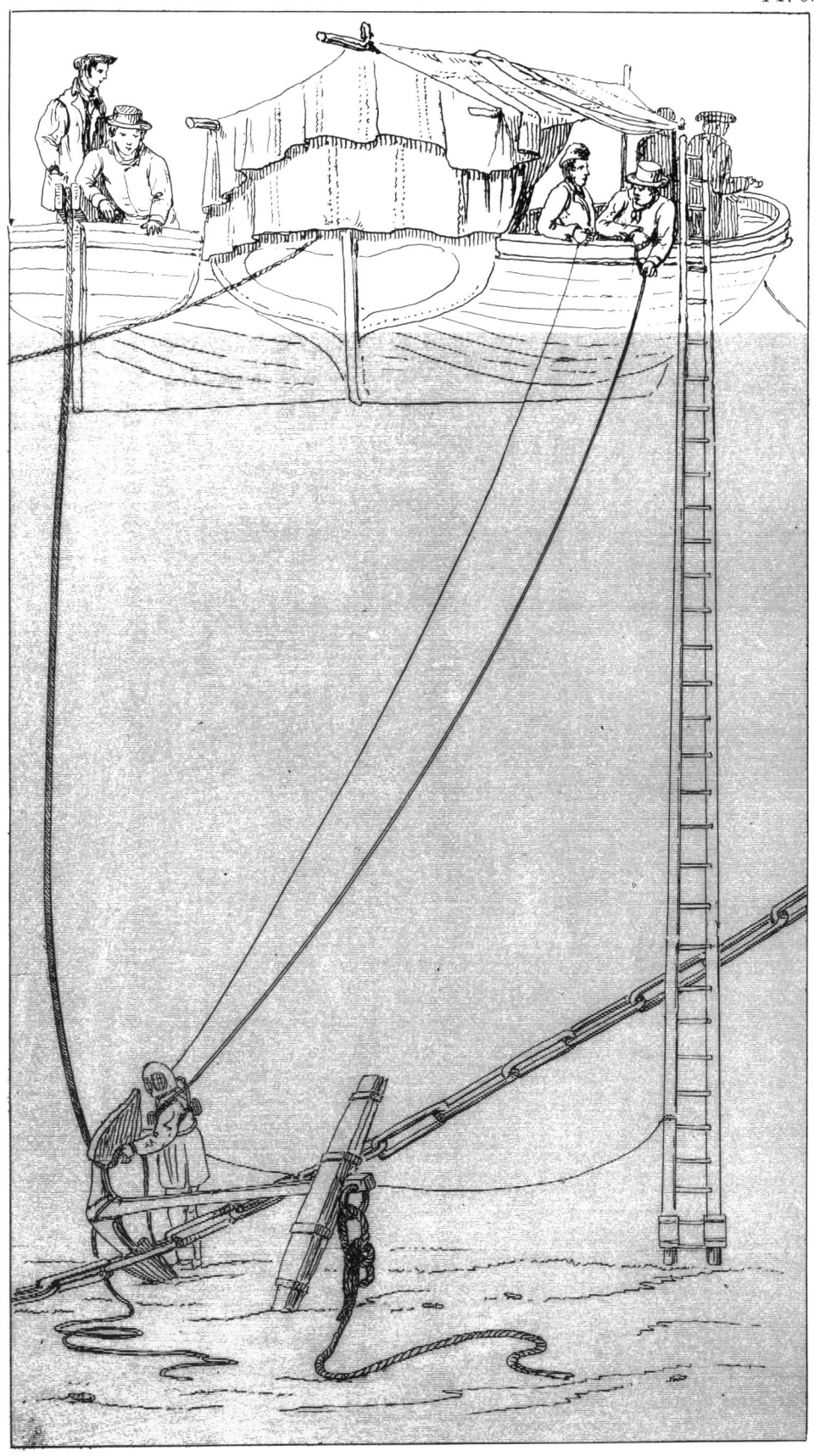

Pl. 6.

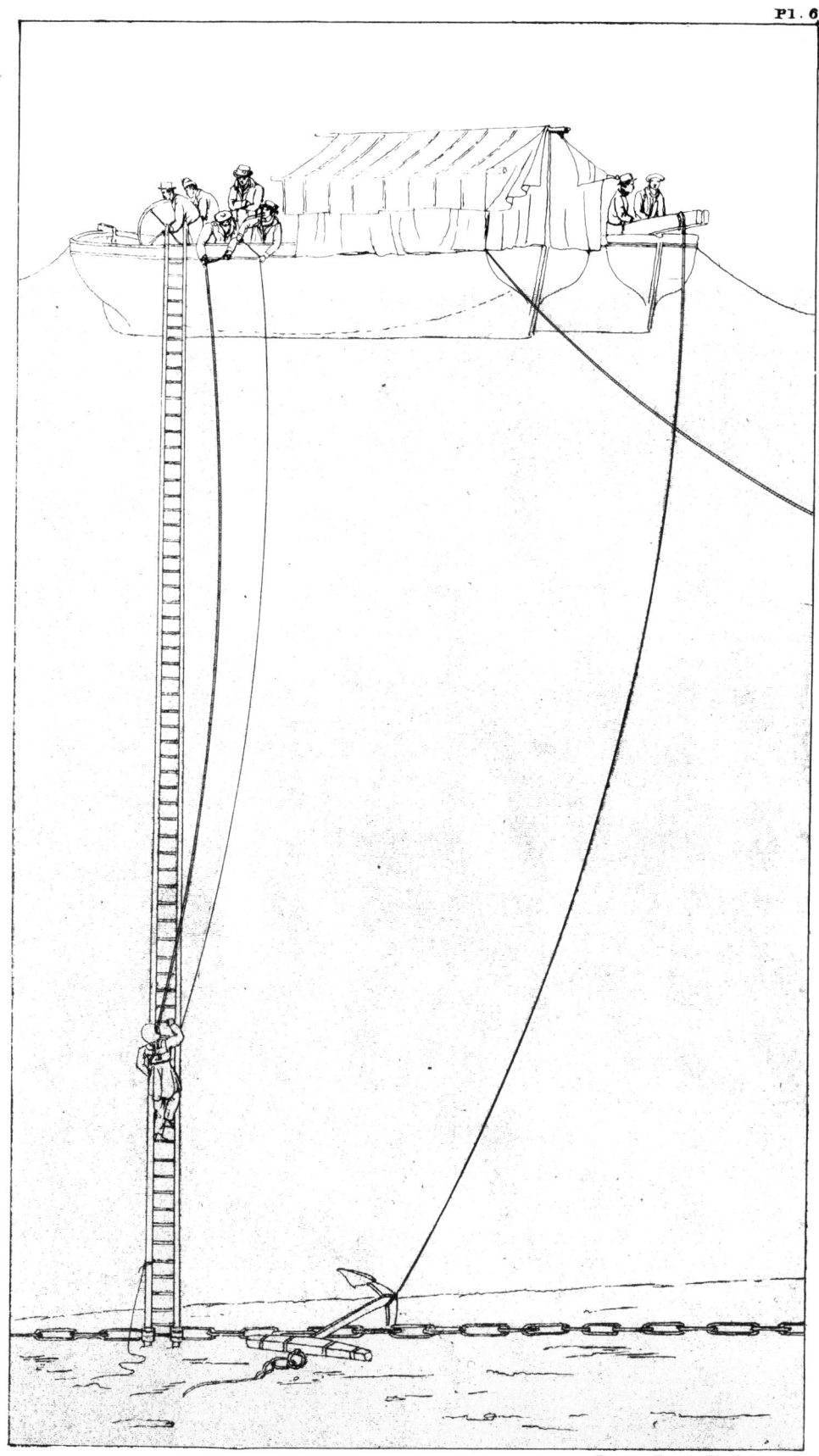

Printed by C. Hullmandel.

Pl. 7.

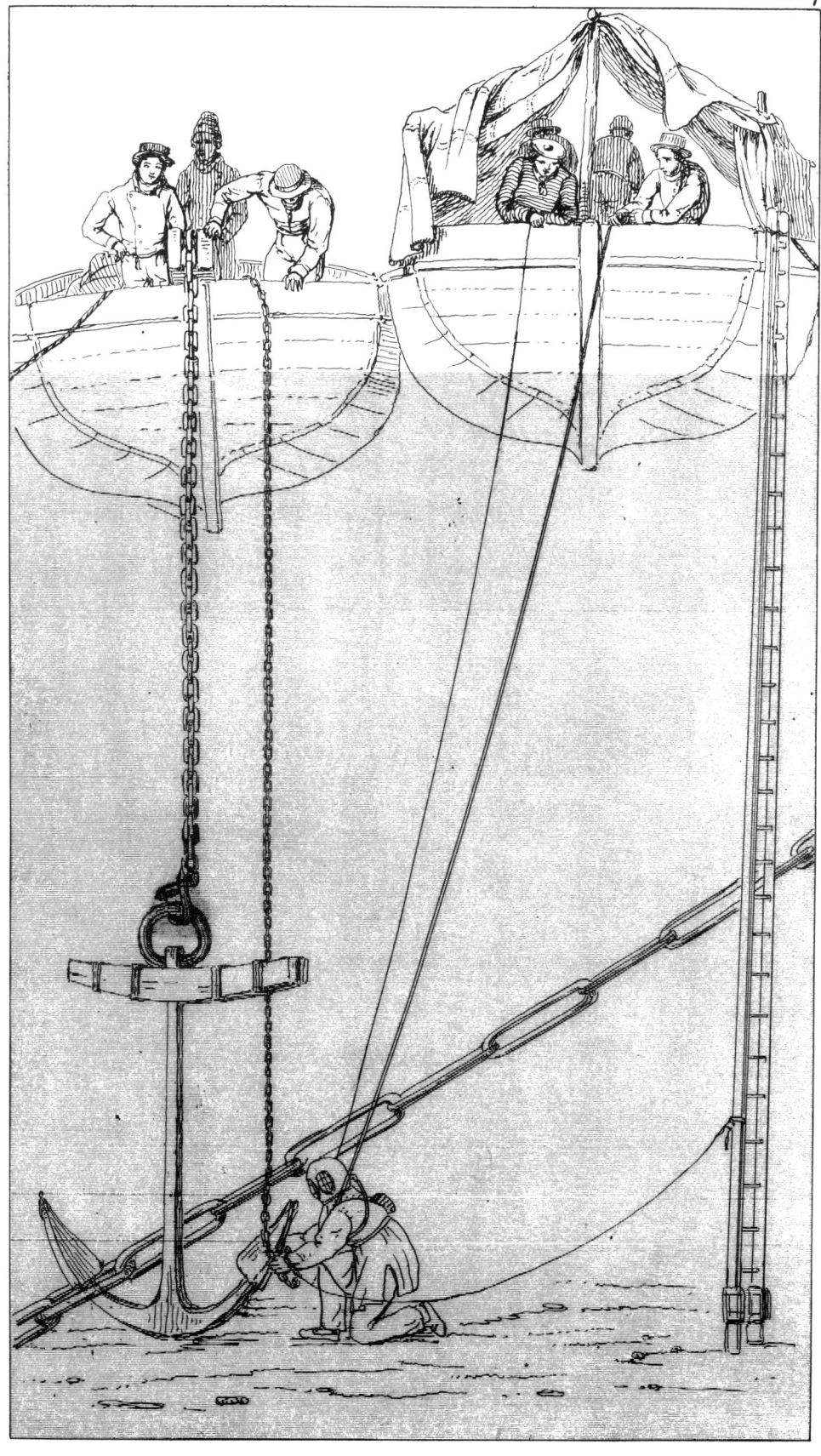

Pl. 8.

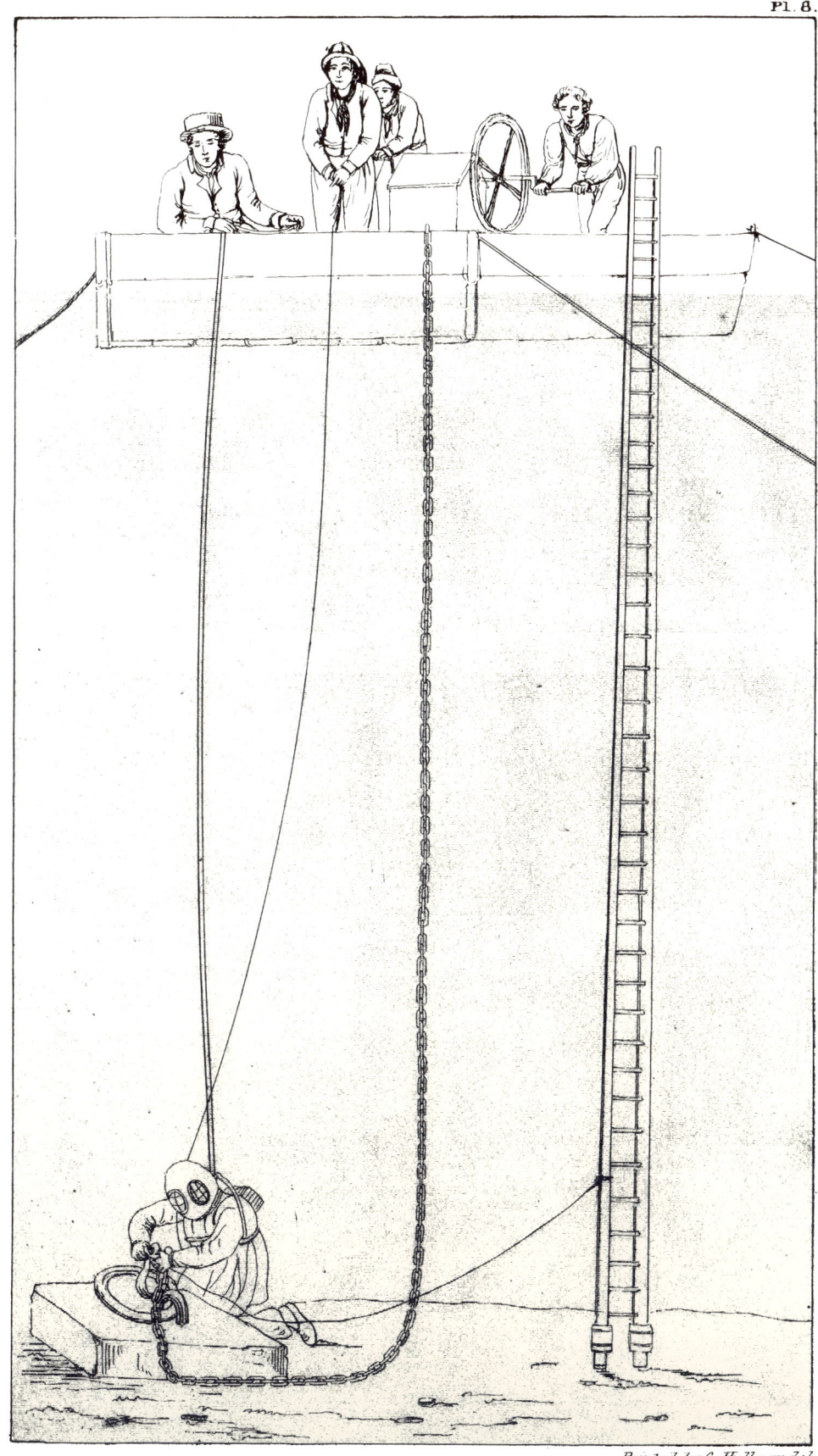

Printed by C Hullmandel

Pl. 9

Printed by C. Hullmandel.

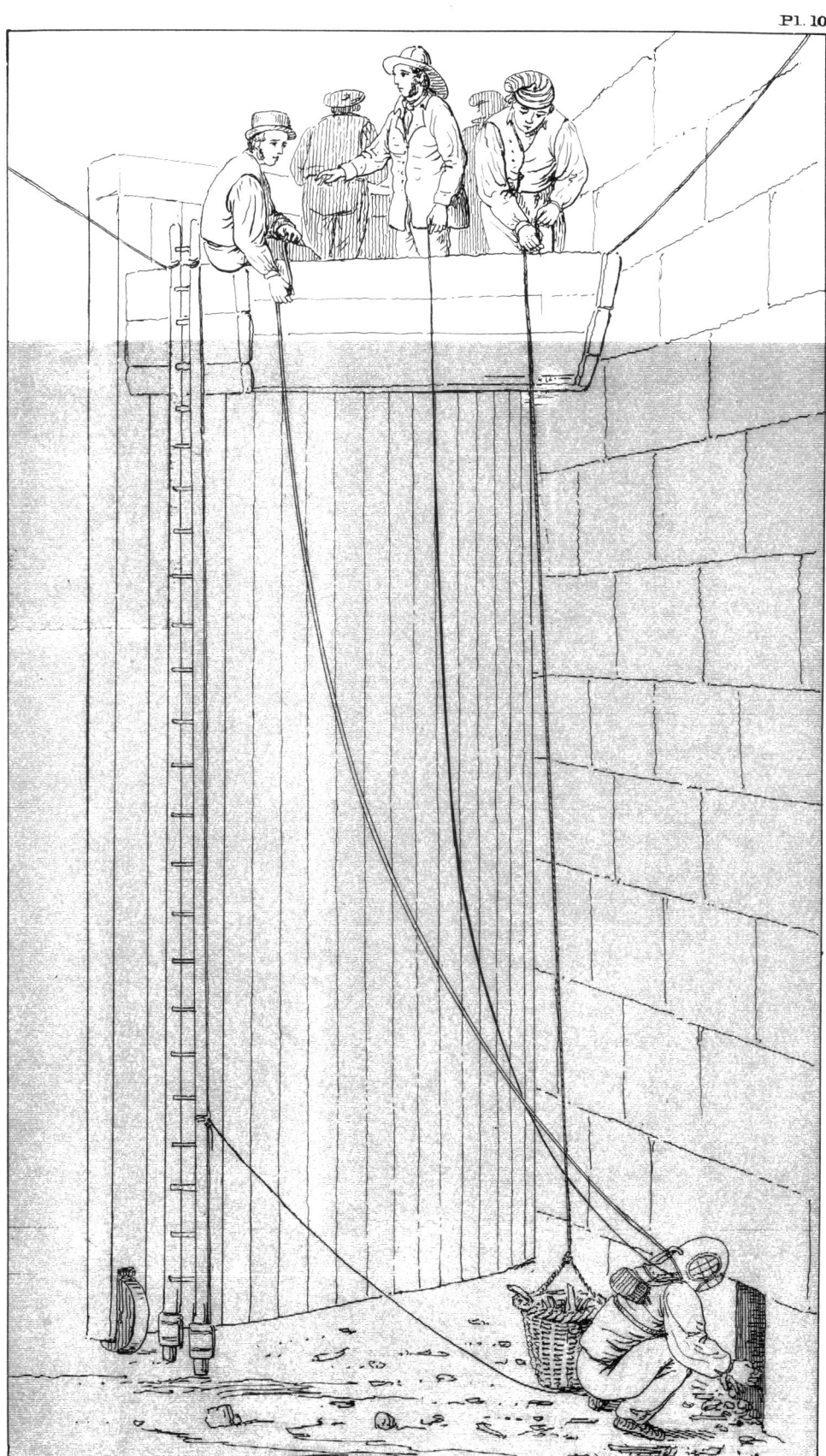

Pl. 10.

Printed by C. Hullmandel.

Printed by C. Hullmandel.

Pl.12.

ENDEAVOUR of MONTROSE

Printed by C. Hullmandel.

Pl. 13.

KENNEDY of CAMPBELL TOWN.

ENDEAVOUR of MONTROSE.

Printed by C. Hullmandel

Pl. 14

Printed by C. Hullmandel.

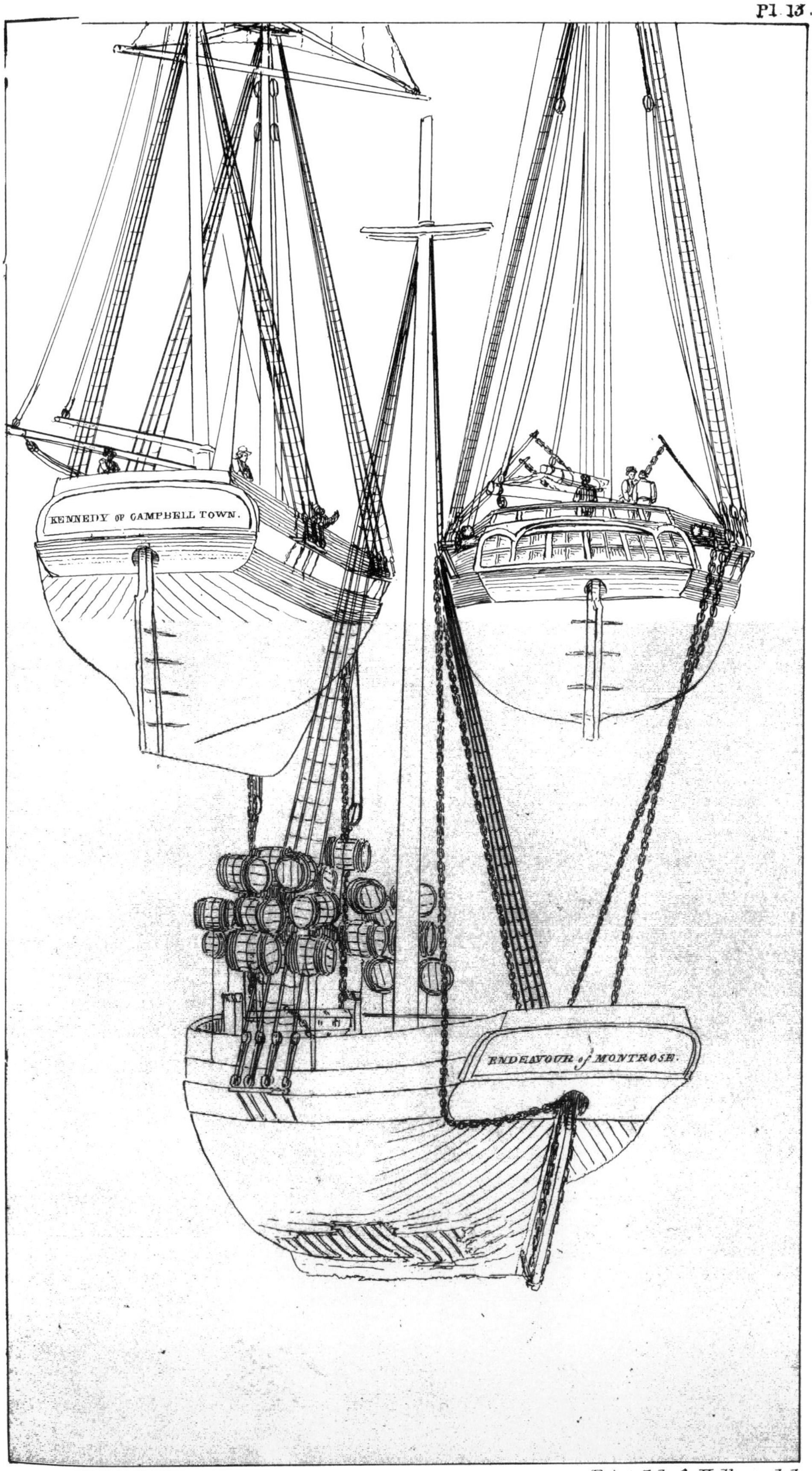

Pl. 15.

KENNEDY OF CAMPBELL TOWN.

ENDEAVOUR of MONTROSE.

Pl.16.

Printed by C. Hullmandel

Pl. 17.

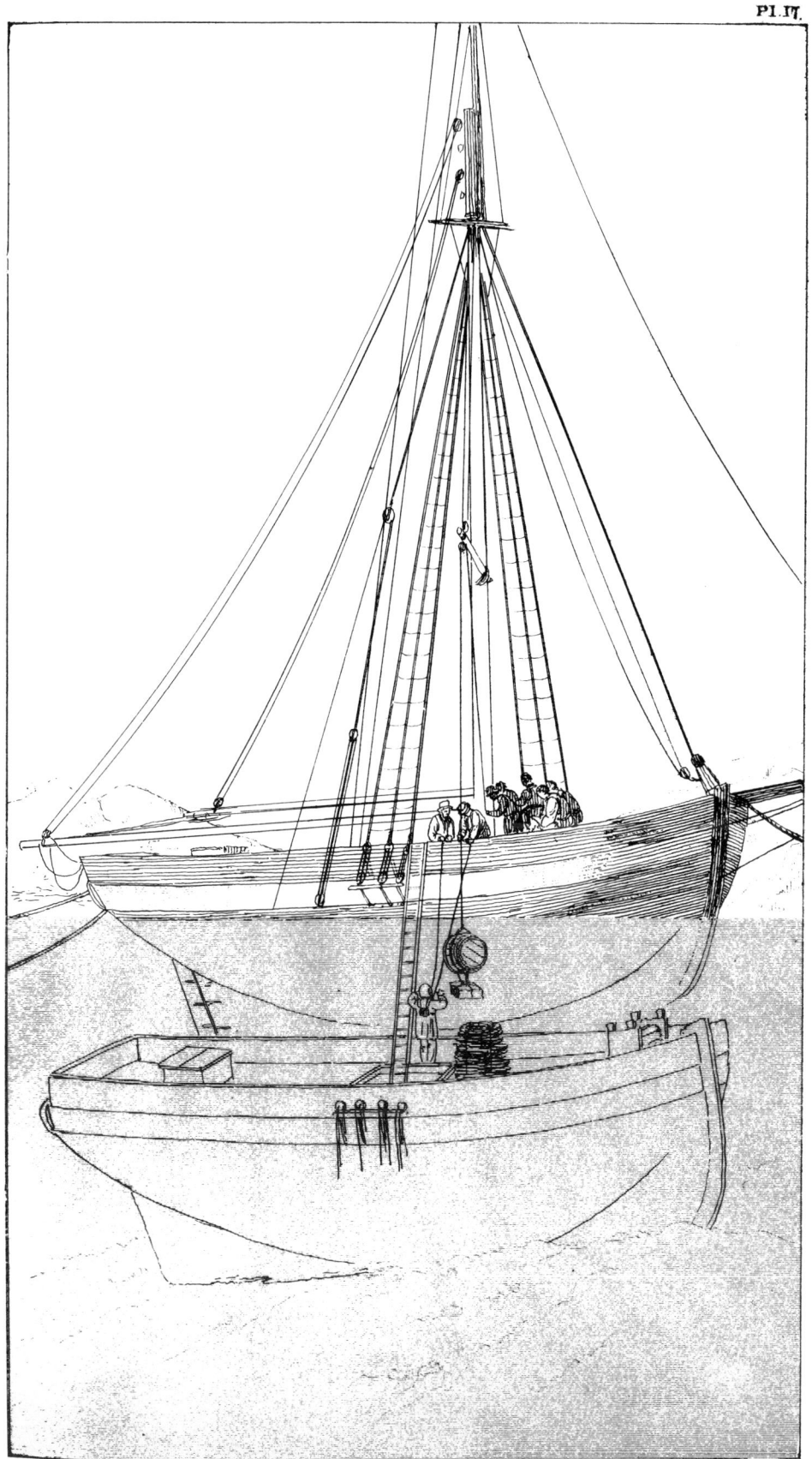

Printed by C. Hullmandel.

.

Pl. 18.

Printed by C. Hullmandel

Pl. 19

Printed by C. Hullmandel.